"BLUE SKY AND A BUICK"
THE JOURNEY OF MARY CHRISTIANA HETTLER

Karen Wilkes

Blue Sky And A Buick

Karen Wilkes

Preface by

Katharine Jefferts Schori, Presiding Bishop of the Episcopal Church of the United States

Wilkes Martin Enterprises, Inc.

2012

All rights reserved. No part of this book may be reproduced in any form, except for the inclusion of brief quotations to review, without permission in writing from the author/publisher.

Cover by Darryl Martin

Copyright © 2012 By Karen Wilkes

ISBN 978-0-615-63131-8

In loving memory of my mother, Alberta Viney Wilkes and of Kathryn Wilkes Duffin, my aunt, who also happened to be my High School English teacher.

This book is dedicated to Layke, Dorian and Kayla

CONTENTS

Preface　9

Introduction　15

Rules Are Rules　25

Christ Church Gets a Make Over　29

Strong Roots　39

The Call　55

Women's Work in the Church　65

Sober, Honest and Godly　75

Set Apart　81

Home Means Nevada　107

Love and Marriage　143

The Church Was Blind but Now It Sees　171

Preface

Women's work has been variously disparaged and exalted in the history of the church, but it continues to be the backbone of most ministry done by and in the church. Women were among the last to witness the crucifixion, and the first to report the resurrection, yet they have been systematically excluded from positions of official authority for most of the 2000 years of Christian history.

Karen Wilkes tells the story of one such vital example, a deaconess in the wilds of rural Nevada in the middle part of the 20th century, a woman who had a profound influence on the writer and on many others.

Mary Christiana Hettler's vocation as a deaconess was really to be a catechist, community organizer and evangelist, even though those terms would have been unlikely in the 1930s when she was trained and set apart as a deaconess. The role of the diaconate (an emblem and icon of Jesus' servant ministry) began to be recovered from the early church tradition only in the late 19th century, and the first women were set apart as deacons in The Episcopal Church in the 1880s. Men had been ordained as deacons all along, and permitted to marry in this Church. Most male deacons expected eventually to be ordained priest, though there were a few stalwarts who understood their vocation as primarily diaconal. Women were "set apart" – explicitly not ordained — and were required to remain single, although widows could take on this ministry.

Deaconesses and women church workers in the early and middle part of the 20th century were largely volunteer missioners, poorly paid, often working solo and in difficult circumstances. In the eyes of the church, they modeled what it means to be a servant of all, and moreover, what it then meant to be a woman in service, taking orders and direction from a priest or bishop. Wilkes notes trenchantly that the women saw themselves as church professionals, increasingly frustrated by church rules prohibiting them from preaching or distributing communion. The conflict between those two views was an important prod in the long search for women's full parity in the offices, orders, life, and governance of the Church.

Mary Christiana Hettler is a foremother for all Christians who seek to live out their vocations in the church and in the world. Karen Wilkes has told her story with grace, wit, and insight, as well as creative scholarship. Her story offers a challenge to today's church: how are we responding to what God is already up to in the communities around us, rural and urban, nearby and far away? Who will go, and how will we be challenged to serve, wherever we are?

The charge from the Bishop of Chicago which framed Mary Christiana Hettler's "setting apart" as a deaconess in 1935 still resounds with the reasons why Christians set out to serve others:

> "We are all members of one another." If the evils of this world are "to be checked, I believe it can only be done by a Christianity which shall, as of old, flame with passion against every exploitation of the bodies and souls of men, and flame with compassion

for everyone who is sick or old, or poor, or ignorant, or lonely or forsaken or sinful, whether it be one of the teeming ten thousands of half-starved coolies in China, or one of the men and women in the neighborhood..."

Deacon Hettler is a shining example of faithful witness, what Christians call a saint.

Read this as a remarkable biography, as a detective's investigation into the life of a fondly remembered teacher, as an image of what it was like to live, work, and worship in the rural West between the mid-19th and mid-20th centuries, or as a profound witness to holiness and faithfulness to vocation in the face of official rejection. The book will reward all those perspectives, and more.

Introduction

I am proud to say that Pioche, Nevada – a "way past its heyday" and "beyond remote" mining community is my home town. To be even a bit more specific, I was raised there in a house built by a mining company for its management, which overlooked the "boot hill" cemetery, the famous Nevada cemetery wherein lies the remains of the first seventy-six men to die in Pioche with their boots on. This happened, of course, in the 1870s shortly after silver was discovered there.

When I was growing up during the 1950s and 60s, most mines had closed, leaving a few stalwart families who stayed on awaiting better times to come again. Unfortunately, at that time I was yearning for a larger venue in which to spread my wings like Las Vegas, Reno or perhaps I could consider Carson City; but that was not to be for many years, as Pioche remained my destiny.

Much later in life, I learned that there were indeed advantages to growing up in an isolated environment. For instance, one could observe one's fellow man or woman at a close and intimate vantage point, taking up a character study that could last twenty, thirty, or even forty years. A person with an adopted persona can only play a role for a limited period of time without being exposed, especially in a small town like Pioche. A game of charades can only last so long, because it is a game. Therefore, in time, we Pioche-ites eventually saw every wart, mole, and stray hair on our fellow citizens and knew every nuance of their character. There were no secrets.

My study of Deaconess Mary Hettler began when my parents decided that they should send their daughter, me, to the Episcopal Church to learn some about the teachings of the Bible, and, it appeared to me that picking the Episcopal Church was not based on any particular theology, but with the thought that their daughter should be a member of a Protestant denomination. My dad had attended this same church during the latter part of his childhood in Pioche, and my mother had been raised a Methodist. The Episcopal Church was probably the least invasive denomination in Pioche at that time. It seemed to be a "live and let live" kind of church where their daughter was safe to explore the tenets of Christianity, and with luck, attendance there would not provoke too many deep theological discussions. My parents were very nurturing, instructive, supportive and spiritual, each in their own way; and, they were in total lock step on formalized religion – you just didn't need too much of it. Therefore, on most Sundays my dad very faithfully dropped me off at church and picked me up after it was over. My mother did worship with me sporadically, but for the most part church attendance for me was a solitary event.

Pioche is about fifty miles west of the Utah border and the population was and is about fifty percent Mormon, The Church of Jesus Christ of Latter Day Saints, and fifty percent all other denominations combined. My parents had agreed on a course of action to prevent me from entertaining any interest in Mormonism. The first time that I was asked to go to "Primary" with my Mormon girlfriends, my father explained to me that I could go one time, and that I was to enjoy it and have fun, but to never ask again, because I would never be allowed to go a second time. Somehow the way that he presented this, I knew it was law, and I never asked again. The line had been drawn in the sand. That line was, and, I imagine still is always present in this community between Mormons and non-Mormons. It is unspoken, and strangely enough, citizens on both sides have learned to live with it and to skirt around it when needed — no one ever fights over religion in Pioche.

Occasionally, someone wanders over the line from one side to the other, and this can cause some friction within families, but it is usually accepted in time. I do not ever remember a weapon being drawn in Pioche over religion – over some other disagreements like mining claims, but not religion.

It was in this setting that I strangely found my spiritual home in the Episcopal Church, which would sustain me throughout the rest of my life. I loved everything about this little church in Pioche – how it looked, whitewashed and stalwart perched precariously on a 45 degree grade on the side of the hill, defying gravity and still maintaining a "so what" kind of attitude; how it smelled, musty with no apologies; and how the bell sounded ringing over the entire community at 10:00 a.m. every Sunday. I liked its sparse aesthetics – a simple altar – no frills. I loved the rituals and the rhythm of services and the recitation of ancient creeds and prayers. Yes, I felt you could count on this little church to go the distance. And, I found an environment where I could safely worship with all my questions, such as what happens to the souls of Pygmies in darkest Africa. Since I have never changed in that regard, I am still worshiping with my questions sitting by my side every Sunday. In fact, I have found that if you stack them correctly, they really don't take up that much room.

It was here at Christ Episcopal Church in Pioche that I began my character study of Deaconess Mary. This study was, however, occurring in my subconscious, as I was only nine or ten years old. Actually, I was a little afraid of the Deaconess, as she always dressed in her deaconess habit and most certainly ran Christ Church with much authority. She had her deaconess rules for the behavior of children and was not afraid to take any of us kids to task if we got out of line – which she accomplished most of the time by giving us the deaconess look. It was a very stern look, and we all thought she might have a direct line to God and maybe to Jesus, and we better shape up or lightning might strike us. It was clear that she had a kind heart, but there was no mistaking that we kids were there to learn about Christianity and the Episcopal way of expressing that, and maybe not always in that order.

Deaconess Mary was adamant that we all needed to be confirmed by age 12, accompanied by the proper education, and that we all needed to go to Camp Galilee in the summer. That seemed a pretty good trade-off to me. So, if Deaconess Mary wanted me to be confirmed, I was willing, and I picked up my questions and proceeded directly to confirmation.

Of course, later in high school and college, my resolve and religious discipline waned, and I did not see Deaconess Mary for many years, nor did I really think about her. I had new questions to answer, and I had moved from Pioche as had my family. In fact, I was completely stunned when this subconscious study entered my conscious mind in the third quarter of my life. All of a sudden, I started thinking about the life and impact of a deceased woman whom I had only seen once or twice since I graduated from high school.

"Why?" I asked myself repeatedly. All I can say is that Deaconess Mary Hettler kept entering my mind over and over until I decided that I had to talk to my husband about this kind, but strong-willed apparition. Was this bordering on some type of mental disorder, I wondered? After some discussion with Darryl and with several other friends, I came to the conclusion that someone should write a story about the Deaconess, as her life was quite interesting with several unusual twists and turns. But, who?

I spent months trying to think of someone from Pioche whom I might be able to convince to write this story. But, try as I might, the right person did not come to mind. I eventually faced the fact that the Deaconess was living in my head, not that of any others, and she was not showing any signs of moving out soon. With further introspection, I came slowly to the realization of how she had impacted my life and had been a role model for me. I am indeed a slow learner, but eventually I started to see the bigger picture of how pioneer women in every field have paved the way for women like me to succeed in all careers, including business, sports, and in institutions of all types — religious and otherwise. Now I knew that her story must be told, and that I needed to muster the courage to dust off my forty-year-old English degree, which had been sitting dormant and untended in the far reaches of my mind, and move forward with gusto. After all, that's what Deaconess Mary would have done!

Not really knowing where to start, I made a few phone calls and sent e-mails to parishioners at Christ Church Pioche asking for any documents they might have pertaining to her ministry, and then I thought maybe I could find out where she was trained and a little about her family, as this was going to be a short story or a short research paper – that sounded attainable.

Initially, the parishioners at Christ Church didn't think they had anything. And the Diocese of Chicago where she was trained didn't seem to have anything either – too long ago, etc. However, one person in Chicago told me to call the Episcopal Women's Project. More calls led to more calls – and no documents. The story could have ended here.

But one day, I received an e-mail from someone at Christ Church saying a box of Mary's things had been found at the church. Wow! "Could I have the box?" I e-mailed back with haste. I was able to pick up the box on a trip to Lincoln County and found that it was an unlabelled cardboard box, and that it had been sitting in the church's storage area since 1961. It was a treasure trove of her writing, mementoes and photos. Very shortly after that, I got a phone call from Richard Seidel, a retired Episcopalian in Chicago, who had been working as a volunteer with the archives of the Episcopal Diocese of Chicago. Someone had given him my number and told him of my phone calls. He remembered seeing the name of Mary C. Hettler and promised that he would look for anything he could find about Mary and about the Deaconess training school which she had attended. A whole package of information arrived within two weeks. I now had more information than I had dreamed possible. I was no longer writing a term paper. It needed to be a book. Deaconess Mary had spoken.

With much trepidation, I started to trace down her family members and her step children, all of whom so graciously allowed me to interview them and dialogued with me in the most candid and loving way. These interviews continued with fourteen more people who had known or worked with Mary at various times of her life. And, in every interview, without exception, a spiritual catharsis occurred between interviewer and interviewee, as Mary was our subject and her spirit embraced us.

This book is my most humble attempt to impart to others the incredible spirituality and life's journey of one of God's special messengers who walked briefly with me and quite obviously changed my life. We can't go forward successfully without understanding our past and understanding the lives of those pioneers who blazed the trails we now see as paved. Hopefully, sharing the story of Mary Christiana Hettler will bring additional clarity into your life as it has mine.

Chapter 1

Rules Are Rules

"Aunt Mary, do you still wear your white cuffs?"

"No, dear."

"Does this mean that you are not in the Church anymore?"

"No, the white cuffs are to show other people that you are in the church; but you can still be in the church without the white cuffs."

The cuffs, niece Anita Dodson El-Jamal recalled, communicated something important. "The white cuffs she wore were starched so stiffly that when she took them off at night, they used to stand up on the dresser like obedient little soldiers. But, later when I visited her in Nevada, she was no longer wearing her cuffs."

For twenty-four years Mary Christiana Hettler had proudly worn a dove gray dress accompanied by a starched white wimple (hat) and equally starched white cuffs paired with black low-heeled pumps — the official "habit" for an Episcopal Deaconess. She dressed this way seven days a week, year after year, as it showed others that she was about the work of God, and Deaconess Mary was on duty twenty-four/seven.

A clear vision of her purpose, accompanied by a single-minded nature, made her an ideal prospect for any type of missionary work, and doing this work made Mary a happy woman. She always walked with a jaunty step, head held high with the posture learned from a mother who expected her daughter to move easily in the high society of Chicago, marry well and produce above average grand children.

Perhaps her mother should have given more thought to the naming of her firstborn baby girl, because Mary Christiana, carrying a name loaded with Christian symbolism, seemed to march in a straight line directly into the arms of the Episcopal Church, much to the serious dismay of her socially upwardly mobile mother.

Mary had plenty of energy, a work ethic instilled by second generation German immigrant parents, good organizational skills, and a good education and training for her chosen field. In other words, Deaconess Mary was a veritable "God machine."

Some folks might have felt that on occasion her methods were not as tactful as should be fitting for a Deaconess, but no one, and I do mean no one, ever doubted the seriousness of her calling.

But, on May 15, 1961, after twenty-four years of faithful service to the Episcopal Church, Mary's world tipped on its axis and was never to be the same again. She was relieved of her duties by Bishop William Godsell Wright, who had been consecrated May 1, 1960, in the Diocese of Nevada, which at that time was a missionary Diocese of the Episcopal Church of America. Mary had made a decision to marry James W. Bradshaw of Elgin, Nevada, and she had sent a letter of resignation in accordance with protocol to her Bishop, who resided in Reno, the official seat of the Episcopal Bishop of Nevada.

About three days later, enough days for the Bishop to have received the letter via the mail delivery system in rural Nevada, Mary heard a knocking on her front door at a very early hour of the morning. Somewhat startled, she went to the door, and behold, she saw a very red-faced, angry, and agitated Bishop. Bishop Wright had driven through the night the 429 miles from Reno to Pioche on Highway 50, the loneliest road in America, to confront Mary and inform her in no uncertain terms that he would not accept her resignation because she was deposed. She had one week to remove her belongings from the basement apartment of the church, where she had resided for the past twelve years. After all, rules were rules, and Bishop Wright, himself a married man, was in charge of making sure all rules of the Episcopal Church were adhered to in the missionary Diocese of Nevada, and this included the outpost of Christ Church in Pioche, as well.

Pioche was at that time and is a town of about 500 people – the seat of Lincoln County, which could be one of the more sparsely populated counties in the nation. It is about 100 miles of open road from anything in any direction — north, south, east, or west. As you can imagine, the Deaconess post would be a difficult position to fill in Deaconess Mary's absence, but rules are rules, and no Deaconess in the Episcopal Church could be a married woman, not even in a high desert outpost in the outback of Nevada.

Chapter 2

Christ Church Gets a Make Over

When Deaconess Mary arrived in Pioche, on February 1, 1949, she was replacing another Deaconess, Esther Matz, who was retiring. She, like Mary, resided in the daylight basement of Christ Church. The church, formerly a miner's union hall, was built in 1917 against the side of a hill. The entire town had been built on several adjoining hills just below the mines, as miners needed to be able to walk to work.   When you enter the church's Sanctuary from the upper street, the basement is below, with one wall of the lower level against the hill and the outer walls having windows and a door leading out to the side of the hill. As you can imagine, since it was a former union hall, the church is just a plain wooden clapboard building. Here is how Mary described it in her notebook upon arrival to her new post:

"An old grey building badly in need of paint, cold and drafty. Church was furniced (sic) with oil burner stove, many loose chairs – hand made

lectern, prayer desk, and altar. Beautiful altar linens and silver chalice set and Bran Cross and 6 candles, pump organ given by Dr. Quincy Fortier – later electrified by him. Louver floor – large room used for community and church dinners or other activities – had a long table with about twenty chairs covered with complete white covers. Looked like a meeting of the Klu Klux Klan.

"Large kitchen with gas water heater and oil heating stove. Sink on one side of room and dish shelves on far side of room. Roller skates needed to get around in. Door opened into kitchen with table just inside. No one got beyond the kitchen – they just sat down at table.

"Living Room – small – had day bed, chair and door to bedroom with steps and large recreation room. Bathroom on far side of building – like an ice box in winter."

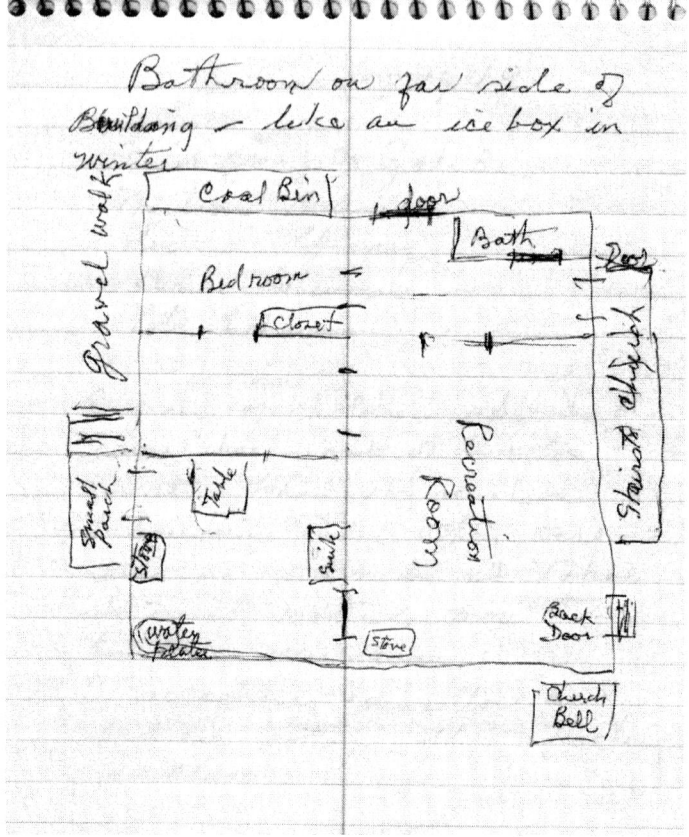

Deaconess Mary, with her organizational skills, an iron will, and "Depression-era" work ethic, started her meticulous top to bottom makeover of Christ Church, turning it into a starched white building inside and out. Of course, she had almost nothing to work with in the way of materials, but that never held our Deaconess back. Deaconess Mary wrote in her notebook:

"Early on in my training for a Deaconess I was advised when beginning a new assignment to note things which stood out as needed doing and list them. It would take time and money to correct these needs, but if listed one would not get use to living with them and forget to see they were done."

Her list for the betterment of Christ Church was as follows:

>*Paint church*
>
>*Put in walk and flowers*
>
>*Clean (Leona Cheeney) and refinish church floor*
>
>*Get pews to replace chairs in church*
>
>*Put up wall board in recreation room*
>
>*Move kitchen*
>
>*Add bedroom and put bath between bedrooms*
>
>*Get rid of coal oil stove in church*

Later in her notes, it's obvious that things got done.

"Mr. Brown – Christ Church Las Vegas – came up and installed oil furnace for church. Old propane water heater was replaced when kitchen was moved. Bill Orr arranged for electric water heater. He and Bill Webb moved plumbing for new kitchen. I built cabinets in kitchen and bathroom and did some painting.

"Charles Miller of Caliente came up and painted interior of church proper with paint donated by Rosevere Paint of Las Vegas. United Thank Offering helped with paint for exterior – Parcel Post sale and other fund raisers covered that. Combined Metals furnished the scaffolding.

"Pete Cole walked the ridge of the roof and put up new stove pipe. Rex Bentley cut wood and glass so I could frame eight 'Autobahn' pictures to hang in recreation room. Painted it a shocking pink – a real change from dull grey. The beaver board lining on side and end wall really cut out a lot of cold. The old wains-coating had shrunk so much one could see daylight thru the walls. Four Monroe folding tables were purchased. These served for numerous dinners and other functions including church *school. The oil stove in lower inside corner had to be filled from barrel out the back side door and lighted each time a meeting was scheduled. Both Boy and Girl Scouts used this room."*

As a child attending this church on Sundays, I always marveled at Deaconess Mary's resplendent collection of African violets on glass shelves in the kitchen window of her basement apartment. Not much grows in Pioche, so beautiful flowers always stand out against this back drop of rocky hills thrust upward from the desert floor — rocks on top of rocks, some valuable and some not so valuable. To gaze upon these tropical flowers was thrilling for me.

My mother, having been raised on a dairy farm in Yuba City, California, was forever trying to change the landscape around our house, which also sat on the side of one of the adjoining hills overlooking Boot Hill, from one of an "early miner" look to a Napa Valley vineyard design. Oh my goodness, what a time she had of it — the high hopes of importing plants every Spring to watch most of them die from frostbite during the winter, or from malnutrition due to the rocky and heavy mineralized soil . She could have given in to just planting the few plants that could possibly make it, like snapdragons, flax, lilac and hollyhock bushes, but not my mother. She kept trying to beautify the desert, one tropical plant at a time, which she would import every summer from Yuba City when we visited my grandparents. Living in Pioche was never for sissies. It was a town built for single men to stake their claim, get rich, and leave. This was not a town designed for women and children, but come they did, and some stayed, as did Deaconess Mary and my mother, joining a group of stalwart women determined to bring civility and beauty to this rough and tumble mining community.

The Deaconess shared her cozy apartment with all of us at church meetings and always for coffee hour after services every Sunday. We children looked forward to the Kool-Aid and cookies in the kitchen, and marked our maturation by the date when we would be allowed to sit with the adults on the Victorian antiques in the living room that had been donated to the church by a parishioner. As a girl, I concluded that the day my mother allowed me to wear nylons (the precursor to panty hose) must be the day that I could casually saunter into the Parish living room and perch on the red velvet upholstered Victorian settee with the lion's head arms and lion's paws legs. I was positively stunned by the beauty of this matched pair of antiques, to the point that when the church decided they needed to be re-upholstered in 1986, and that this would not be a correct usage of parish money, I offered to buy them. These proud lions now adorn the entry of my home and are a great reminder of fond memories of the Deaconess and the little Episcopal Church that has bravely held onto the side of that rocky hill and delivered steadfast service to God's children in Pioche. I can still hear Deaconess Mary's slightly shrill laugh in the kitchen while she busied herself with cakes and cookies during the coffee hour.

As you can see, Mary's home and her ministry were tightly tied together in this once booming, but now declining Nevada mining town, making the visit from the red-faced bishop devastating. The war was over, and lead, zinc, and tungsten were no longer in demand for the war effort, lowering the price per ounce to the point that was hard for the mines to turn a profit. After twelve years, the human forces of longing for companionship and a family had taken hold of Mary's heart. However, there was no wiggle room in the policies of the Episcopal Church regarding women in ministry. Ordained men could be married, but not so for women.

Canon 50, approved by the General Convention of the Episcopal Convention of 1943, spelled it out:

"Sec.1. A woman of devout character and proved fitness, unmarried or widowed, may be appointed Deaconess by any Bishop of this Church, subject to the provisions of this Canon. Such appointment shall be vacated by marriage."

Deaconess Mary Christiana Hettler had a life-changing decision to make – continue her ministry as a Deaconess or marry James W. Bradshaw, a lanky, handsome, soon-to-be-divorced cowboy with three minor children, ages twelve, ten, and seven.

Chapter 3

Strong Roots

Mary was born May 11, 1911, to Neva May Harney and Christopher Frederick Hettler in Lubbock, Texas, where her father was working on the ranch of one of his brothers. Mary's grandfather and his brothers had immigrated to the United States from Germany through the port at Galveston, Texas, and several of them had started ranching in Texas and settled there. Frederick's father, however, had moved north and raised his family in Marion, Indiana, where Frederick was educated, graduating with a college degree in accounting. The two branches of the Hettler family stayed in touch, and whenever one of the city boys needed toughening up, they sent him back to Texas to work on one of the family ranches. So Frederick moved back and forth several times from Indiana to Texas, on one trip meeting Neva May Harney and marrying her in 1910.

Neva gave birth to Mary Christiana in 1911, Ruth Harriet in 1912, Helen Louise in 1922, and Betty Jane in 1926. Anita El-Jamal, the daughter of Helen

Louise, has shared her recollections of the family history for this book. There had been a Mary Christina, a Mary Christian, or a boy named Christian in the Hettler family for several hundred years. Thus, the name of Fred and Neva's firstborn was Mary Christiana. The name had no religious imperative to the family; it was strictly a family name to be honored. Neva was a small woman with a "Scarlett O'Hara" waist, who loved clothes, liked to be the life of the party, and longed for city life. Fred became the equivalent of a regional director for World Book Encyclopedia, and the family moved many times to various parts of the West, depending on where World Book needed Fred Hettler's supervision. Eventually, Fred heeded Neva's longing for the city and he moved the family to Oak Park, Illinois, a suburb of Chicago, probably when Mary was about ten years old. Since all four daughters are now deceased, we don't have a full record of those years. Years later, Fred, tired of travelling, became an accountant for Seidman and Seidman in Jasper, Indiana, where he and Neva lived the rest of their lives, passing away in 1960 and 1963, respectively.

Mary took after her mother in build and interests, being smaller boned and interested in clothing, sewing, housekeeping, etc. As she grew into adulthood, she was always perfectly groomed, with coat buttoned up when she went out, appropriate hat, and always white gloves, making her mother very proud. But, Mary inherited her father's sensibility and was more reserved. Unlike her mother, she never raised her voice. Her sister Ruth had more of a stocky German build, and was a tomboy, caring not a bit how she looked when she left the house. As happens sometimes with sisters, Mary and Ruth had trouble understanding one another and were not close as adults. Mary ended up closer to her sister Helen, who became an accountant and worked for many years with their father, ultimately taking up the role as head of the family and taking care of many problems for her sisters, for which she was well-equipped due to her father's careful tutelage.

Several photos of the two girls, Mary and Ruth, taken in Oak Park, show very well dressed children indeed. Mary's niece, Anita El-Jamal reminisced that her grandmother Neva "used to take her daughters to Marshall Fields on Thursdays to 'high tea,' where they would sample the teas and pastries and watch the weekly fashion show. At the end of the fashion show, Neva and the girls would march directly to the fabric department, where Neva would purchase fabric to use in her next creation for herself or one of her daughters, copying a garment that she had just seen on the runway. She was an expert seamstress, but would buy extra fabric to take to a milliner for matching hats. She also used the services of Mr. Hoee, a local tailor, for especially difficult tailoring."

Neva had scoliosis, and the result was one shoulder and one hip were higher than the other. She and Mr. Hoee collaborated on designing her dresses to camouflage this impairment by never installing zippers down the back of the dress, but under one arm, or using buttons down the front of the garment. It was under this attention to detail that Mary and Ruth learned to sew and to design clothing. Later in life they would both design and make jewelry as well.

Many women during this era made their own clothes and those of their children out of necessity, as store-bought items were always more expensive. Sewing was also a wonderful outlet for artistic creativity, an art which we are losing today. My own mother was much like Neva, ambitious for her daughters and loaded with creative energy needing an outlet. A good Friday night for my mother was an evening with a bag of chocolate-covered raisins and the latest issue of Vogue magazine. There was no "Marshal Fields" in Pioche, of course, nor was there a Penney's or a Sears. So when it came time for me to attend a Junior Prom in the early 60s, my mother kicked into full gear — it was "four on the floor with full gas." A shopping trip to Las Vegas was planned immediately to look for The Dress. This was not quite like shopping in Chicago, but it was the best we could do in one weekend. In those days, clothing and variety stores did not stay open on Sundays, so the plan was to drive to Las Vegas, a three-hour drive, early Saturday morning, shop all day for The Dress, spend the night in a motel on Las Vegas Boulevard North (someplace like "The Hitching Post"), and drive back to Pioche on Sunday with The Dress.

We arrived in Las Vegas about 10:00 a.m. when the stores opened, and we shopped in every store up and down Fremont Street again and again trying on dress after dress. They were all too mature looking for a sixteen-year-old-girl. It was Las Vegas, and they were selling cocktail dresses on Fremont Street, not prom dresses! Perhaps there were other stores, but we could not seem to find them and it was 3:00 p.m. Just short of despondency, my mother took me to a small soda fountain counter in a department store for a Coke and to ponder this dilemma. After about ten minutes of silence — we were both wearing down, and discouragement was starting to set in – my mother looked at me and said, *"I can see that I have to make this dress. We have an hour and a half. The fabric store will be closing at 4:30, and we need to pick out a pattern and the material. Let's go back to the store where you liked the dress with the handkerchief hemline, and I will see if I can figure out how it's constructed. Then on to the fabric store, and we better hurry."*

Back down the sidewalk to the dress shop – by this time I was getting blisters from my dress shoes, which didn't get worn very often, but were definitely the appropriate attire, according to my mother, for a shopping trip in Las Vegas. We asked the sales lady once again if I could try on the dress with the "pointy hemline overskirt," and my mother and I crowded together into the dressing room with the dress. My mother sat on the small stool provided and turned that dress every which way four or five times. She whispered so the saleslady would not hear, *"I've got it, let's go."* I was wide-eyed and in a state of shock. Could my mother really pull this off? But, what choice did I have at that point, but to follow her blindly and hope for the best? She had never led me wrong before. We practically ran to the fabric store, threw open the pattern books and started with a process of elimination: *"Do you like this top or this one? Do you like a scoop in the back or a square? Do you like a higher neck in the front or a lower neckline? Do you like collars? "* and on and on and on. She picked out several patterns from which she would use parts of each, and then we started looking for the fabrics, *"What color do you prefer? Look at the silver thread in this fabric – see how it shimmers – wouldn't that be pretty on the top?"* She paid for the patterns and many yards of three different fabrics. We walked out of the store, and it was 4:20.

My mother made me a beautiful dress using three different white fabrics, featuring an overskirt with a handkerchief hemline, which was just right for a sixteen–year-old girl to wear to a prom at Lincoln County High School. She did pull it off, indeed. This was the pioneering spirit of rural Nevada women at that time. They would not be defeated, nor let society leave them behind. They would just pedal harder.

Under the rearing of Fred and Neva Hettler, all four of their daughters would attend college and have careers. None would follow the exact path outlined by their mother, but each would reach out to identify and follow her individual destiny.

 Niece Anita El- Jamal, recollects that sister Betty Jane, the baby of the family, was fifteen years younger than Mary. She obtained a degree in chemistry from Eastern New Mexico University and a second degree in archaeology from the University of Arizona. While in Arizona, she met a fellow student, George Hunt Williamson, an anthropology major, and they were married. Williamson did not graduate and was in fact disqualified by the University of Arizona in 1951 on the grounds of poor scholarship.   However, he later became famous and somewhat infamous for (1) claiming that he and Betty Jane were with several others when they met an extraterrestrial being by the name of "Orthon" on November 20, 1952, at Mount Palomar, California, and (2) claiming that he and Betty Jane discovered the "Nazca Lines" near Machu Pichu in Peru, where they had a second encounter with "Orthon." Williamson wrote several books on this subject, always using Betty Jane's credentials to lend credibility to his work. We don't have any independent work written by

Betty Jane, so it is hard to say how much she participated and intellectually bought in to Williamson's claims.

The Nazca Lines are located in the arid coastal plain of Peru, 400 kilometers south of Lima. They cover about 450 square kilometers. These lines were scratched on the surface of the ground between 500 B.C. and 500 A.D, and are among archaeology's greatest enigmas because of their quantity, nature, size, and continuity. They depict living creatures, stylized plants, and imaginary beings, as well as geometric figures several kilometers long. It is believed that they had ritual astronomical functions, as well as being used by farmers to know and control the meteorological agrarian cycles. They were designated a UNESCO world heritage site in 1994.

 At some point Williamson changed his name to Michael d'Orbrenovic and later claimed to be of Yugoslavian royalty. Despite his lack of credibility, it is clear that he is known as a fore-runner, along with Alec Hidell and several other cronies, in molding and expanding the contemporary UFO mythos. A "Google" search for George Hunt Williamson makes for some entertaining reading.

Betty had given birth to Mark Frederick Williamson in 1953, and within a few years the three of them were living in Peru. Apparently, George Hunt Williamson was publishing articles and leaving the country repeatedly to give speeches at various conferences in Europe and the U.S. during this period. He had left Betty and son, Mark, in an outlying area in Peru in the care of an elderly native couple while he travelled to Egypt on a speaking engagement. Betty had contracted rheumatic fever as a child and was not physically strong. The lack of nutritious food and the stark environment (they were several days' burro ride from any medical attention) took its toll on Betty, and she died of malnutrition on August 11, 1958, and was buried in Linca, Peru. Her mother, Neva, went to Peru and brought Betty's son back to the U.S., where he lived for a number of years with his Aunt Ruth, Mary's sister, until his father remarried and came to retrieve him some years later.

Sister Helen married Jack Dodson and had three children, Carolyn Louise, Carl Frederick and Anita. Helen's mother, Neva, was not supportive of this marriage, as Jack was from Oklahoma and did not have a formal education. But eventually, as he did well in Indiana as a contractor installing commercial sprinkler systems, Neva began to realize what a fine man he was and became an ardent fan. Anita's first daughter, who died at five month's gestation, was named Mary Christian, to carry on the Hettler tradition. Even though all three of Helen's children were raised in Jasper, Indiana, and were not able to spend much time with their Aunt Mary, they did know her and have shared wonderful memories for this book. When Anita got married, Mary gave her the first cross that she had worn as part of her deaconess habit, to be the "something old" for Anita to wear at her wedding. Anita felt a very strong kinship with her Aunt Mary and says, *"She was my favorite aunt. I have fond memories of sewing with her. Boy, could she sew. If you could make a house out of a piece of fabric, she would have one."*

Ruth, the second born, attended college with the intention of becoming a phlebotomist. She was not able to continue this work, as she discovered that she was "shade blind" and could not distinguish between the subtle differences in the various shades of blood. This led her to a degree in nutrition. She worked many years for a dentist in Chicago and for the County Welfare Department in Missouri. Although married twice, Ruth did not have children, but she and her second husband, Glen Sallee, did help to raise her nephew, Mark, after his mother died in Peru. Ruth, like Mary, also loved to sew, make jewelry, and work with any type of crafts. According to Anita, Aunt Mary could always make a very little amount of anything go a long ways, but Ruth had her beat in that department. Ruth was definitely the queen of "thrift," going so far as to save the unused back side of letters for re-use in her genealogy projects. Now, that's thrifty.

As far as the nieces and nephew know, Helen, their mother, was an Episcopalian, Ruth was maybe a Methodist, and they think that their grandmother, Neva, attended the Episcopal Church and later Church of Christ, but was probably not a member. Frederick, their grandfather, was most likely Lutheran. What we do know is that Mary Christiana was baptized September 12, 1915, at St. Paul's Episcopal Church in Lubbock, Texas; confirmed June 8, 1924, at St. Peters Episcopal in Chicago, Illinois; and entered Deaconess training school on September 2, 1935, graduating from there on June 6, 1937. We know this for certain as these events are written and listed in Mary's own handwriting, found in personal papers left in an unlabeled cardboard box in storage in the little white clapboard Episcopal Church in Pioche. Anita, her niece, also remembers her mother telling her that Aunt Mary was very fond of the Episcopal Church she attended as a teenager in Chicago, probably St. Peter's, and was always at the church participating in youth events and any other possible activity that was going on. The Episcopal Church was surely the place where she felt she belonged, as she for the most part committed herself to the church at age fourteen or fifteen. Her mother refused to acknowledge this commitment and of course thought it was just a phase, but later the family realized that it had truly been an adult commitment from the beginning.

Fred, Neva, Ruth and Mary 1922

Mary at age 19

Mary age 11 – Chicago   Mary at age 24

Chapter 4

The Call

Mary Christiana Hettler graduated from high school in Oak Park, Illinois, in 1930, and on September 2nd, 1935, she entered the Chicago Church Training School. During her time there, she also attended Lewis Institute, taking classes in social service, and The University of Buffalo, where she took courses such as Marriage and Family, Speech, Psychology, and Human Biology.

"The Chicago Church Training School," which would be Mary's home for the next two years, had begun eighteen years earlier as an experiment when Bishop Anderson admitted Miss Hettie G. Lyon to train under Deaconess Fuller, who was then engaged in City Mission work. Lyon became a deaconess in 1919 and devoted herself to that type of mission work until her death in 1937. Between 1920 and 1924, the Diocese of Chicago then trained five other women for this work.

Three women were next admitted from the Dioceses of Ohio, Milwaukee, and the District of Oklahoma, one being Miss Helen Boyle, the first graduate to enter missionary work in the foreign field. Between 1930 and 1938, seven others were admitted as well as an additional eight women who used their training as a platform for other occupations such as teaching, nursing, or entering a sisterhood. Through the years from 1921 to 1938, all the students lived at Chase House with their expenses being paid either by themselves or by friends, family, parishes, or women's auxiliaries, such as the Daughters of the King.

The Chicago Church Training School's brochure states, "*From the beginning much importance has been attached to sound social service training, and courses in Case work, etc., are taken at University College with field work under the United Charities of Chicago. Training for parish work is given by the Deaconesses at Chase House with field work in selected parishes. A short course in hospital work is required.*" The course was divided approximately into thirteen months of practical work and nine months of academic work with two summer vacations of one month each. "*The two years or more of preparation is the student's opportunity to build up a rule of life for herself; all Church privileges are available to her, and she has freedom to form her own habits of devotion. The expense of the course is $500 a year, and the minimum length* *of the course is two years. Necessary qualifications are good health and good sense; character is supremely important."* The goal of the training school was to send out Deaconesses or lay teachers competent to instruct and prepare children or adults for confirmation and communion, using this as an evangelism tool to grow the church.

Chase House, the home of the Training Center at 211 South Ashland Boulevard in Chicago, was formerly the sedate and elegant home of John Wilson and his two sisters, Mrs. King and Miss Margaret Wilson. Originally built in 1855, on the corner of Ashland Boulevard and Adams Street, the home was in a fine neighborhood adjoining the Church of the Epiphany. However, by 1920, the area had changed from a residential one to a miscellaneous grouping of medical and dental schools, hospitals, fraternities, and rooming houses. The rapid deterioration of the neighborhood created a demand for more social work than could be given by the church, so when the Wilson property became available for sale, the Diocese of Chicago purchased it for $20,000 to be the first outreach center of the Episcopal Church on the west side of Chicago, joining its outreach ministries with those of the existing parish.

Chase House became the home of Mary Hettler from Sept 2, 1935, to June 6, 1937. She worked hard, enjoying the discipline that was demanded by this type of life. She honed her skills, and the time came for Mary to officially apply to her bishop to become a full-fledged deaconess, going out into the world to do the work of God. Mary was fit and she was ready, having no doubts about her purpose in life. Unfortunately, her mother, Neva Hettler, was not amused. She was very much against this direction her oldest daughter was taking, and according to niece, Anita El-Jamaal, was very vocal about her opinions. This would cause a rift between Mary and her mother that was lasting, and most communication between Mary and her family would come through her father, Fred, or through one of her sisters from that time forth.

Chase House - Chicago

"E are all members one of another. And if Communism with all its materialism, all its atheism, all its class warfare, all its resort to force, is to be checked, I believe it can only be done by a Christianity which shall, as of old, flame with passion against every exploitation of the bodies and souls of men, and flame with compassion for everyone who is sick or old, or poor, or ignorant, or lonely or forsaken or sinful, whether it be one of the teeming ten thousands of half-starved coolies in China, or one of the men and women in the neighborhood of Chase House . . ."

—The Bishop's Charge, 1935.

REV. HAROLD HOLT, RECTOR   MRS. JOHN Y. BAKER, SECRETARY   GEORGE H. CLARK, ORGANIST AND CHOIRMASTER

Grace Church
Oak Park, Illinois
924 Lake Street

September 20, 1935

The Rt. Rev. George Craig Stewart, D.D.
65 East Huron St.,
Chicago, Ill.

My dear Bishop Stewart:

    Miss Mary Hettler of this parish has been accepted by the Deaconess' Training School at Chase House as a candidate. She is a girl of fine character, very much interested in church work and with, I feel, a definite call to that work.

    Deaconess Fuller tells me that a letter from you to her is necessary. Will you please issue such a letter that she may be fully accredited ?

    Sincerely yours,

    Harold Holt

1936 – Mary Hettler, left   After being "Set Apart"

Mary Hettler – Left

Mary Elizabeth Hyde – Center

Madeline Dunlap - Right

Chapter 5

Women's Work In The Church

Women had been the last ones at the Cross and the first ones at the Tomb on Easter Day, according to the New Testament, and they had assembled with the Apostles in the Upper Room while awaiting the Ascension. As the church then spread from Jerusalem, we hear of the good works of Dorcus; of Lydia who was baptized with her entire household and whose home became headquarters of the Church in Thyatira; of Priscilla, a leading teacher in the Church in Ephesus; and Phoebe, who Paul commends to the Church in Rome.

After the days of the Apostles, the Order of Deaconesses grew, especially in the Eastern Church, where at one time there were forty deaconesses attached to one church in Constantinople.

Deacons were first mentioned in the Acts of the Apostles, "*as a group chosen from among the faithful and charged with a servant ministry, distributing the elements at the Eucharist, visiting the sick and the imprisoned, and taking food and clothing to widows and orphans."* They always worked under authority, first that of the apostles and later that of local bishops. There were men and women serving in this capacity, with the most notable woman being the New Testament Phoebe.

Deaconesses appeared during the fourth century in the writings of early church fathers including Ignatius, Tertullian and Cyprian, and canons regulating deaconesses were passed at the Ecumenical Councils of Nicea and Chalcedon. Researchers even discovered ancient liturgies for the consecration of deaconesses, but by the fifth century with the passing of time, women began to move from the deaconess role into monastic communities of sisterhoods, which continued for many centuries.

Historical church scholarship in England hit a new high during the 1800s, which is commonly referred to as the "Oxford Movement." Several of the leading tractarians during this period had founded sisterhoods and were generally supportive of the monastic tradition, but as they began to delve deeper into accounts of the beginnings of Christianity and the development of its ministries, they discovered the very significant role that deacons had played in the early church.

In 1862, the Reverend John Saul Howson, the dean of the Chester Cathedral in England, published an exhaustive study of the New Testament concluding that, *"The argument for the recognition of deaconesses as part of the Christian ministry is as strong as the argument of the episcopacy."* On the strength of this research, Bishop Archibald Campbell Tait of London admitted Catherine Elizabeth Ferard to the order of deaconesses in 1882, and she in turn founded the North London Deaconess Institute for training other candidates. By 1871, a majority of the English Bishops including the Archbishop of Canterbury had signed a statement defining a deaconess as, "a woman set apart by a bishop under that title for service in the church."

A concurrent interest in the role of women deacons was also brewing in the American Episcopal Church. In fact, in 1858, four years prior to the publishing of Houson's research in England, Maryland's Bishop Whittingham had "set apart" the first seven deaconesses in the Episcopal Church using the Kaiserswerth model developed by Pastor Fliedner of Westphalia, a province of Prussia. Pastor Theodor Fliedner was a German

Lutheran minister who had been originally influential in German prison reform. However, after spending some time with the Mennonites in the West Indies, he became empowered to open a school and hospital in 1836 in Kaiserswerth, now an area of Dusseldorf, for the training of Lutheran deaconesses as nurses in order to effect reformation in the field of health care. He had become known in Europe as the founder of deaconess training programs. His most famous pupil was Florence Nightingale, an English health care reformer who visited his program and then later returned in 1851 to complete the program and graduate in nursing. The success of the Kaiserswerth model proved that such orders could be developed in a Protestant denomination without leading to excesses that "low churchmen" in the Episcopal Church feared from the possibility of sisterhoods.

The reference to "low churchmen" refers to a philosophy in the Episcopal Church that emphasizes the separation from the Roman Catholic traditions leaning more towards the Protestant aspects of the Episcopal Church. Conversely, "high churchmen" continue to practice many traditions that are much more akin to those of Roman Catholicism, such as the support of monastic orders for men and for women.

Many articles and books have been written analyzing distinctions between the Catholic and Protestant views of women in ministry, and most authors agree that the pervasive power of the images of women as either "Mary," meaning the Virgin Mary, or "Eve," the evil seductress, have shaped the Catholic hierarchy's collective attitude toward women and toward the women's views of themselves. On the other hand, in the Episcopal Church and other Protestant denominations, the image of Mary never received the veneration it had in the Roman Catholic Church. Thus, Episcopal women had a somewhat easier time of choosing from a wider variety of role models and were not as locked into the "domestic motherhood" image; however, this is not to argue that the path of these women in the Episcopal Church was straight and smooth sailing – far from it.

By 1920, various models of women's ministries had evolved, including the order of deaconess, missionary workers, wardens, and headmistresses of various institutions and some sisterhoods. During the preceding sixty years, women had transformed the Episcopal Church by fostering a support system conducive to the expansion of ministry in establishing and operating schools, hospitals, orphanages, and neighborhood social

service centers. However, the National Episcopal Church had gone through a major reorganization in 1919, and in the process had definitively excluded women from the ecclesiastical political structure. The women were doing herculean amounts of work, but were officially excluded from representation in the decision making process of the church.

Women had won the right to vote in America with the 19th Amendment to the Constitution ratified on August 18, 1920, but it would be five decades before women would have the right to vote on matters in the Episcopal Church. It wasn't until the General Convention of 1970 that for the first time, twenty-eight duly elected women deputies took their seat at the General Convention, having both voice and vote.

Some historians feel that the evolution of women's ministries in the church directly coincides with the rise of the "social gospel." In *The Rise of the Social Gospel in American Protestantism*, Charles Howard Hopkins traces the movement from its beginnings in the preaching of a few isolated churchmen in the 1870s to its maturity in the optimistic period right before World War I. He contended that four currents of thought during the Gilded Age combined to bring about this theory: *"(1) the complacency of conventional institutionalized, orthodox Protestantism, (2) the attempt to reconcile the truths of Christianity with the new science, (3) the evangelical hope and fervor that had inspired the previous generation's crusade against slavery, and (4) the Unitarian school that challenged both the presuppositions and the ethics of conservatism."*

Amid the unsettled economic conditions and industrial strife of the 1880s, these factors combined to produce a growing emphasis on the church's responsibility to the betterment of society – a call to work for the coming of the kingdom of heaven on this earth. According to Hopkins, this sense of responsibility led to the development by churches of institutions such as orphanages, nonprofit hospitals, and social service centers in poor neighborhoods. A new social theology was forged that created a direct ethical influence upon the concept of God, man, sin, and salvation. For instance the concept of sin was expanded to include not only personal vices but the collective forces of evil, meaning that society as a whole is

responsible to address corporate sins. This new theological stance had a lasting effect on the Protestant attitude toward sin.

In the Episcopal Church and most other denominations, the labor force used to implement the social gospel, providing social services to the disadvantaged, was composed overwhelmingly of women, and the church was able to offer this abundance of services because these women were willing to work for long periods of time as volunteers or at extremely low wages. They were living the theology of the social gospel through their actions, not their words.

This was the philosophy that was taught at Chase House, and the philosophy that Mary C. Hettler would carry forth with her into the greater world for the rest of her life. Everything she did from this time forward can be seen through the lens of her training at Chase House. This servanthood type model for the behavior of women would prevail in business as well as all other institutions until the late 1960s, when the women's movement really started to gain traction, leading to significant change in the attitude towards the work of women.

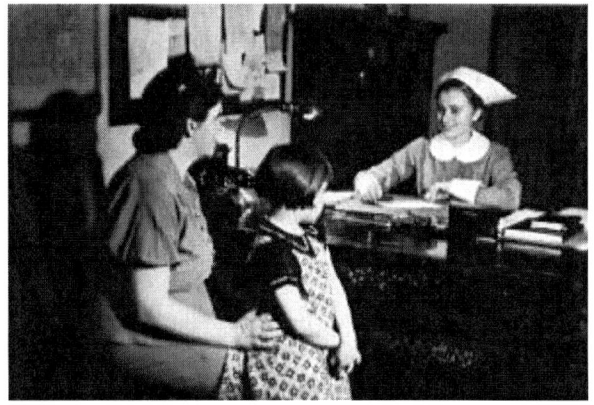

Deaconess Mary at work at Chase House

Mary 1940 – Racine Conference

Chapter 6

Sober, Honest, and Godly

During this period, the office of deacon for a man was generally an interim position to becoming a priest. Few men remained deacons for an extended period of time. On the other hand, the position of deaconess had been shaped by the Church's hierarchy, who believed that a women's highest calling was to marry, and that if she did so, she could not serve both God and her husband. Therefore, a man's marital status had no bearing on his position as a deacon, but the Church canon that addressed the role of deaconess clearly stated that the appointment as a deaconess shall be vacated by marriage. This was hotly contested between the deaconesses and the Church at large. The deaconesses felt that they were making a lifetime commitment and that the "vacated by marriage" language was an undermining feature of that commitment and an erosion of their vocation. They felt belittled by this, and we can certainly see through this conflict surrounding the double standard between women and men and their respective rights and duties as deacons versus deaconesses a spark of the women's movement beginning in the Episcopal Church.

The role of men as deacons was to assist the Priest with church services, helping him distribute Holy Communion, reading Holy Scripture, and in the absence of the Priest, baptizing infants and also preaching, if approved by the Bishop, and lastly searching for the disadvantaged in the Parish. The deaconesses, however, had no liturgical functions. Their duties were to *"assist the Minister in the care of the poor and sick, the religious training of the young and others, and the work of moral reformation."* The man was ordained a deacon by the Bishop, who placed his hands on the candidate's head saying, *"Take thou Authority to execute the Office of a Deacon in the Church of God committed unto thee";* whereas, the woman was *"set apart"* by the Bishop, who shook her hand saying, *"For the service of our Lord we receive thee, to be henceforth known and called by the name and title of a Deaconess in the Church of God."* The deacon was given authority, and the deaconess was accepted for service. Eventually, the deaconesses did receive a "laying on of hands" versus the "handshake" used in the earliest "setting apart" services, and Mary did receive the laying on of hands when she was "set apart."

A continued tension prevailed between the view of the Church hierarchy and the women themselves regarding the role of deaconess. Mary Sudman Donovan in *The Deaconess Papers* archived, at the Diocese of Chicago bore witness to this when she wrote:

"The clergy saw the deaconess as a religious extension of the ideal of true womanhood – a woman would be pious, pure, submissive, and domestic, who would simply substitute obedience to the priest or bishop for obedience to a husband. Contrastingly, the women saw the deaconess as a professional church worker – trained in Scripture and theology as well as housekeeping and nursing – who would exercise a vocation of service to the Lord Jesus Christ through the institutional Church."

The deaconesses had been trained by other deaconesses and saw themselves as initiators, but the clergy expected them to work as directed, creating a dichotomy that continued to cause conflict for the better part of the twentieth century.

Some clergy were more enlightened than others and did understand the women's view of their role.

Archdeacon of New York C.C. Tiffany expressed in a 1896 sermon,

"Sisterhoods have been permitted in the Church; Deaconesses are an order of the Church....This woman's diaconate, like that of men, is a regular ministry, owing allegiance to the Bishop and parish Rector....In this order there is the constant recognition of the Deaconess by the Church and the Church by the Deaconess. In it we have the Church's benediction of woman as the minister of Christ...a recognition and approval of all the noble work by which Christian women have enriched the world...So this order of Deaconesses is to teach the sacredness of women's work for Christ, by giving it a place in the regular ministry of His Church."

On December 14, 1937, the members of the Standing Committee of the Diocese of Chicago officially voted and testified that Mary Christiana Hettler was *"sober, honest and godly, and that she was a communicant of this Church in good standing, and possessed the qualifications which fit her to be 'Set Apart' as Deaconess."*

DIOCESE OF CHICAGO

Deaconess

To the Right Reverend GEORGE CRAIG STEWART, D. D., Bishop of Chicago:

(Date) DEC. 14, 1937

We, being a majority of all the members of the Standing Committee of the Diocese of Chicago, and having been duly convened at Chicago, Illinois, do testify, that from personal knowledge or from certificates laid before us, we are well assured that (Miss) MARY CHRISTIANA HETTLER is sober, honest and godly; and that she is a communicant of this Church in good standing; and we do furthermore declare that, in our opinion, she possesses qualifications which fit her to be Set Apart as Deaconess.

IN WITNESS WHEREOF, we have hereunto set our hands this 14" day of December in the year of our Lord 1937.

(Signed) Edw. Randall

W. F. Towley

George _____

Arthur _____

_____ Ward

Gerald L. Moore

Chapter 7

"Set Apart"

On December 21, 1937, at 10:00 a.m., a Thursday, which we might expect was a cold and blustery day in Illinois, Mary Christiana Hettler was "set apart" by the Bishop of Chicago, the Rt. Rev. George Craig Stewart at Grace Episcopal Church, 924 Lake Street, Oak Park, Illinois. She was presented by The Rev. Edwin J. Randall, the sermon was preached by the Very Rev. G.G. Moore, and the Gospel was read by the Rev. Gordon R. Galaty. Mary was 30 years old.

> The Bishop of Chicago
> will set apart
> Miss Mary Christiana Hettler
> to be a Deaconess of the Church
> on Tuesday, December the twenty-first
> [St. Thomas Day]
> in Grace Church, Oak Park
> at Ten o'Clock

After a vacation of ten days, on December 31, 1937, Mary was hard at work, having accepted a position as assistant to the Head Resident of Chase House and then later became Acting Head Resident working under Helen M. Fuller, who was a major force in the Deaconess movement during this period and who had opened the training program in 1917. Mary could not have had a more honored role model than Deaconess Fuller. Mary honed her skills under the careful tutelage of this visionary woman, learning about management, hiring of personnel, meal planning, buying, housekeeping, and educational and recreational group organization of all age groups.

Not knowing where this path would lead her, on October 1, 1939, Deaconess Mary left the comfort of this very structured way of life and the familiar faces at Chase House and was reassigned to the Town and Country Council, a division of the Diocese of Chicago, where she began her rural ministry. In a Diocesan newsletter of September 1939, it was reported:

"Deaconess Mary Hettler is to be released from her duties at Chase House on October 1 to take over

work in the Town and Country Council area, according to a recent announcement by Archdeacon Norman B. Quigg." (a colleague with whom she would correspond into his very old age) . "In her new post, Deaconess Hettler will act as general assistant to the rural archdeacon and to the priests in charge of mission stations. She will also supervise the Town and Country Council correspondence school, in which 400 children in the widely scattered farm homes of the area are enrolled.

 "Her duties will be similar to those undertaken by Deaconess Adams, before the latter's removal to the Diocese of Wyoming."

 In a letter from Archdeacon Quigg to Mary dated October 3, 1939, he states, "Your stipend of $1350.00 a year is in the main paid by the Diocesan Council, although $120.00 of it is an appropriation by the Women's Auxiliary. It is understood that you will own your own car, toward the purchase of which you will receive a gift of $200.00. The auto allowance of 3 cents a mile is paid by the Diocesan Council, your travel being estimated at about 1000 miles a month.

"I suppose I need not remind you of the group insurance plan for deaconesses approved by the Diocesan Council. The requirements are as follows:

"A premium of $10.00 a month provides for retirement at the age of sixty. For one entering at the age of twenty-eight and retiring at sixty, it provides a monthly payment of $40.82; for one retiring at sixty-five, it provides a monthly payment of $59.88. The Council agrees to pay a premium amounting to 6% of the salary received. In your case that will be $81.00. Your annual premium will be $120. Therefore, you will be expected to pay the difference of $39.00. The method whereby you pay this will be in accordance with the plan already arranged with the Treasurer of the Diocese.

"Praying that God may continue to bless your ministry as a deaconess very richly, and with every confidence that you are going to do a grand work on the Town and Country Council."

Six months later Mary writes in the April edition of the Diocese of Chicago newsletter,

"During the past sixteen months, I have driven 40,000 miles visiting the isolated, assisting in *various missions and counseling with students in several colleges and with those from the Diocese of Chicago who are at the University of Illinois. My car takes the worst kind of punishment, pulling through snow drifts, bouncing over rocky back-country roads and carrying me on my rounds in all kinds of weather. There came a day when it rebelled and as much as said it had done its duty. With the help of $150 from the ever-ready Bishop's pence, I was able to make a trade for a new car to carry on where the old one left off.*

"My new car is in harbor grey. A colored gas attendant seeing it casually remarked: 'You all sure nuf got a new car. Ah likes it. She sure am flashy.' A typical rural christening followed. Hence the name, 'Flashy.'

"During the year it has been my privilege to visit in the homes of over five hundred scattered churchmen living in areas remote from established Episcopal churches. Many of these families are from the professional class: Doctors, proprietors of stores and businesses, dentists, druggists, thoroughbred stock raisers, lumber dealers and home owners in thriving communities. They have not left the Church, which has not been evangelistic in its growth and so has not penetrated the small

community. Every visit is a challenge. An opportunity to cheer, to sympathize, to encourage, to share a great joy or sorrow await every call. Seldom before I lift the knocker and the door is opened do I have any knowledge of what state I will find any given family facing.

"One mother met me with tears in her eyes. 'We are so happy to have the things which you have been sending Mary, but Sonny was hit on the highway last week and instantly killed. He was never baptized. I have another son who has not been baptized. I always thought we would have both boys baptized at the same time but it never occurred to me that anything like this would happen first. We must have this child baptized before any other unforeseen thing occurs. Will you help us make arrangements?' A priest in the area was asked to call.

"One name of a young man 23 years of age was all we had had in a community of six thousand in Hoopeston, Illinois. I called with Archdeacon Quigg and found that the young man was in the hospital in Danville. We called at the hospital where we met both him and his mother. Through this one contact 11 church families and 2 individuals were located. This work has been referred to the priest at

Danville, twenty-five miles away. Once upon a time the Church had a mission in Hoopeston – it died about 1911. Through our pioneer work it may be revived.

"These families are anxious to rear their children in the Faith and so the Town and Country Council has come to their aid through the Correspondence School. Children are sent lessons through the mail. Some 200 children are being instructed in the ways of the Church through this method, together with occasional visits from the Deaconess and a priest in the area. For this work the Bishop's Pence again came to the rescue and provided some very necessary cabinets for taking care of the vast amount of religious education materials necessary for this enterprise. The materials are of such a nature and so arranged that they have been most helpful for use with the isolated as well as to the mission clergy and their teachers, many of whom have availed themselves of the privilege of browsing through to make selections for their own schools or classes.

"Travel is an expensive item. Emergencies and additional expenses cannot always be avoided and insurance must never lapse. During 1940 the Bishop's Pence provided $100 toward these extras.

All of this was done to make up some of the difference between the estimated 16,000 miles and the actual 40,000 miles which the Deaconess traveled in carrying out her work. By DEACONESS MARY C. HETTLER"

Archdeacon Quigg, a great mentor to Mary, writes in what appears to be an annual report to the Diocese (undated):

"It was a happy day when Deaconess Hettler, formerly of Chase House, took up her duties as Staff Worker on the Town and Country Council. Her work is (1) to assist the Archdeacon; (2) to call on the isolated; (3) to further among them organizations in likely units; (4) to conduct religious education by correspondence; (5) to gather confirmation classes. …..Calls have been made upon the isolated in the Southern Deanery. In addition, the Deaconess has spent consecutive week-ends in various missions, furthering special objectives outlined by the priest-in-charge. Her traveling is estimated at 1000 miles a month. She has been 'the life of the party' for numerous gatherings of children; social and religious movies have been shown; addresses have been given at Sunday

Schools and special services. Wilmington, Watseka, Fairbury, Paxton, Rantoul, Gibson City, Lacon, Oregon and Mt. Morris are small communities in which are numbers of Church families to be visited. At times the isolated have been traced to hospitals where the sacraments and solace of the Church were greatly appreciated. She also assists in a monthly service at The Home for Widows of Soldiers, at Wilmington. And always in her travels she scans and scours no man's land for scattered and lonely Churchmen. And how eagerly they hail the peculiar camaraderie of religious fellowship!"

After three successful and rewarding years on the Town and Country council, Mary writes in what appears to be an undated resume:

"Following the death of Bishop Stewart and with the advent of a new Bishop the arch-deaconal system was dispensed with and 'rural work' was curtailed. I resigned from the Town and Country work in June, 1941, and for four months temporarily took charge of Chase House. This past year I have been taking special work at the University of Buffalo. Canonically I am still a member of the Diocese of Chicago. My contract with the Vestry of St. Simon's comes to a conclusion

in June and it is unlikely that they will be able to employ a full-time Deaconess.

I would like an opportunity of doing worth-while work either in a Diocesan or Parochial capacity. Please let me know if there are opportunities in your Diocese, or if there are parishes to which you could refer me. I prefer Parish work; one cannot tell about other types of work until they are defined. I use this method of contact, since the church at large seems to have no definite plan of placement….."

These series of letters show the difficulty Mary was having in being placed in a permanent position, and unfortunately this was the case for many Deaconesses at that time. They were low on the totem pole and would always be the first to be let go when budget constraints occurred, and there are always budget constraints in any church. This created a constant worry for Deaconesses, who did not live in communities supported by the Church. They needed their jobs to support themselves, and they had to be willing to relocate at any time to take the next job available.

And on June 17, 1942, Mary writes to Bishop Wallace Conkling, the Bishop of Chicago,

My dear Bishop,

Thank you so much for the letter of transfer. I'm somewhat amazed that the church finds it necessary to describe clergy and deaconesses in the terms of those used in the letter of transfer. Deaconesses may be "difficult" but not "vicious."

I am forwarding the letter today to Dr. Jewell to be presented to Bishop Spencer,

Sincerely yours,

Mary C. Hettler

June 19, 1942

Dear Bishop Conkling,

I am writing to say that I had a very satisfactory interview while in Kansas City. With your permission I shall accept the work of Director of Religious Education at St. Andrew's, Kansas City, Missouri. This work would begin August first.

I hope you will be good enough to send my letter of transfer to the Bishop of Missouri. Perhaps Dr. Jewell of St. Andrew's or Bishop Spencer have written you about this matter already.

I regret that there was no work in the Diocese for me but I wish to extend to you my every wish that the work of the Diocese may continue to grow and prosper under your leadership.

Sincerely yours,

Mary C. Hettler

And on January 20, 1943 Mary writes again to Bishop Conkling:

My dear Bishop,

I hope that by this time you have received an acceptance of my letter of dismissory. It was presented by Dr. Jewell immediately, but through some oversight was not acknowledged by Bishop Spencer.

Following our Parish meeting here Dr. Jewell has announced his intentions of leaving St. Andrew's. He has suggested to his entire staff that we look elsewhere for work in order that we too, may resign with him. I hope that if you know of any available work you will let me know. I appreciate all you have done in the past and am grateful to you. This is a small Diocese and opportunities here are few.

I will appreciate any suggestions which you may be able to offer. I realize that this is a busy time for you with convention just a few days off but I have found this announcement quite an unexpected event which again makes it necessary for me to look for another opportunity to serve the Church.

May I extend to you my best wishes and prayers that you may have a profitable and good Convention.

Sincerely yours,

Mary C. Hettler

Letter to Bishop Conkling dated July 17, 1943

My dear Bishop Conkling:

The first of March I resigned as Bookkeeper and Director of Christian Education at St. Andrew's church. Since that time I have been working as assistant to Dr. Louis Palm here in Kansas City.

At the time I resigned Bishop Spencer advised me to remain here in the Diocese as he expected to have a position opening up in the near future. This has not materialized.

I remember that at the time I talked with Bishop Spencer following my resignation he told me that he had not yet accepted my letter. I am anxious to know just which Diocese I am officially connected with and will appreciate having your opinion in this matter.

I am looking forward to serving in the church in some worthwhile capacity in the near future, but it is difficult to ascertain when and where there are openings available.

My best regards to you and to all those at Headquarters.

Mary C. Hettler

Letter from the Bishop Conkling dated July 27, 1943

My dear Deaconess Hettler

Since Bishop Spencer had your letter so long, we had taken it for granted that he had received you and your name is not listed in the current Journal as canonically connected with the Diocese of Chicago. However, if he has failed to acknowledge your acceptance because of unwillingness to formally receive you, I shall of course consider you canonically connected here until you are placed elsewhere though I do not believe that you should continue indefinitely in secular work and I hope that you will very shortly find a new opportunity of service.

I should think that it would be wise for you to make your availability known to the General Headquarters in New York, which you have probably already done.

Faithfully yours,

The Bishop of Chicago

In 1950, this same Bishop was chosen to head up an advisory commission on *"Work of Deaconesses."* He was an Anglo-Catholic, and horrified at the thought that women might be eligible for the seminary training that was the prerogative of men training for the priesthood. He wanted women workers in his church, but he did not want them educated in the seminaries, so he invested his own time and energy and diocesan resources in order to make a separate place of their own for deaconesses.

The number of students at Chase House had declined, and it was no longer a training center. Bishop Conklin lobbied the House of Bishops for a new Central House for the training of Deaconesses, and it was approved at the 1952 General Convention. Even though his motives were counter to the progression of the position of Deaconesses in the Church, he did save the training program, which was in dire straits by 1948.

Letter from Bishop Robert Spencer of the Diocese of West Missouri dated August 12, 1943:

Dear Deaconess Hettler:

Please forgive delay in this letter occasioned by my moving hither and yon.

Your Diocesan connection is with the Diocese of West Missouri and so appears in the Living Church Annual. It does not appear in the list of Chicago, so you are canonically West Missouri.

As I told you when we last talked, I am sorry you had such experience as you did in Kansas City. So far as I know and believe, there was nothing discreditable to you in any way. I stand ready at any time to give you a recommendation to any position in this Church to which you may be called. There was nothing I could do for you in West Missouri, on account of our limitations in Deaconess work………

Robert N. Spencer

Mary then writes again to Bishop Conkling on August 14th, 1943, probably not having received the last letter from Bishop Spencer.

My dear Bishop:

Thank you so much for your letter regarding my status.

You suggest that I leave secular work. This is my desire but in the meantime I must work – I have no resources on which to live during this ad-interim period.

You suggested that I write "281." This I did early in March and have kept in touch with them through the last few months. I have had several letters from Mr. Samuelson and he in turn suggests that I write various Bishops over the Church.

Certainly "placement" is one of the Church's greatest problems to be met for both ordained and lay workers. I have been in both positions and know how difficult it is to bring workers and employers together. Perhaps the General Convention may offer some solution. I believe Fr. Kelley of "281" is conducting a study of the work among women of the church. No doubt the findings are to be presented to General Convention.

Faithfully yours,

Mary C. Hettler

In 1935, there had been 216 Deaconesses in the United States, and there were four training schools: The New York Training School for Deaconesses; The School for Christian Service in Berkeley, California; The Divinity School, Department for Women in Philadelphia; and the Chicago Church Training School. However, by 1957, there were but sixty- eight Deaconesses, of which forty-one were completely retired, and there were only four Deaconess Candidates. The system for delivering ministry in the institutional churches was in transition.

Written in her own hand, Mary lists her employment during these years as:

10/1/39 to 6/15/41 — Town and Country Council, Chicago

9/17/41 to 7/1/42 — St. Simon's, Buffalo

8/1/42 to 3/1/43 — St. Andrew's, K.C., Mo.

6/1/43 to 8/1/45 — St. Paul's, Grand Rapids, Mi.

7/1/47 to 11/15/47 — St. Francis, Orangeville, Mi.

11/15/47 to 1/15/49 — St. Paul's, Grand Rapids, Mi.

On June 26, 1946, Lewis Bliss Whittemore, the Bishop of the Diocese of Western Michigan, writes to Mary as she had now secured a position at St. Mark's Cathedral in Grand Rapids.

Dear Deaconess Hettler:

This is just a brief line to tell you how happy I am that you are going to be on the staff of St. Mark's Cathedral. The Cathedral, I know, is very happy to have you come and you may be sure of a hearty welcome and, I believe, a most valuable and productive field in which to work.

I am personally glad that you are to be here with us and you may be sure of my hearty cooperation. I am especially interested in your coming as whatever is done at the Cathedral has its influence throughout the Diocese so your position will have more than local significance.

With kind personal regards and in much anticipation of our association in the future, I am,

Faithfully yours,

Lewis Bliss Whittemore

And, on June 23, 1947, Bishop Whittemore writes to Mary:

Dear Deaconess:

Thank you for your nice letter of June 20th. I am very happy that you are to be at St. Francis' Mission and look for great things.

Enclosed is a copy of your temporary appointment, which has just come from New York – so that is that!

I am thinking of you this week at the conference. I do hope that you have good weather.

As ever yours,

Lewis Bliss Whittemore

It is apparent that a working woman in an organized religious institution was up against the very same problem that women were having in any career. They were desperately needed as part of the labor force, but the institutions didn't want to pay them, and sometimes couldn't pay them, as they would always be on the lowest end of the pecking order and, naturally, the first to be let go when the budget demanded further cuts. It is also apparent that politics in institutions is always a factor, even in the Church (or maybe especially in the Church). If at the lower end of the pecking order, one is always vulnerable to any sway in the political structure of an organization – thus, being a Deaconess was a very precarious position in which to be placed.

However, in the middle of all of this occupational chaos, Mary Christiana Hettler, true to her nature, purchased on December 4, 1947, a bank draft for $150.00 from the Michigan National Bank in Grand Rapids, Mi., payable to Rev. John Aaron to be drawn on the Imperial Bank of India, Hyderabad (Sindh), India. Her good friend, John Aaron, was a missionary in India and she knew that John needed this money more than she. She had been sending him small amounts previous to this time, $5.00 and $10.00 at a time, but somehow was able to put this amount of money together and share it with her missionary friend. Mary took the parable of the widow's mite to heart, and there would be many instances all through her life where she shared the little she had, which was never very much, with others. I don't ever remember her talking about stewardship, but she certainly was a living witness to the principles of stewardship to all of us who knew her. She most definitely taught by example. Sometimes it is difficult to pin down the exact influences in one's life. The stewardship of time, talent, and treasure became a key interest of mine many years ago and has continued to be the focus of my volunteer efforts in the Episcopal Church. Did this avocation come from my study of Deaconess Mary? I'm not sure, but it certainly did contribute to it.

Mary had saved a small brochure from the, *"National Conference of Deaconesses of the Church"* dated June 1942. On page 2 it says; *"LET US PRAY: For God's blessing upon the newly consecrated Bishop of Nevada, William F. Lewis, and the Church's work in the Missionary District of Nevada."* Mary was obviously at the conference and quite surely said this prayer along with the other Deaconesses. Little did she know that she was praying for a newly consecrated Bishop who would in 1949, become her boss for the next 10 years, and with whom she would have an excellent collegial relationship, one that she had not had since working under Archdeacon Quigg.

Mary – "Set Apart"

December 21, 1937

10:00 A.M.

Grace Church

Oak Park, Illinois

Chapter 8

Home Means Nevada

Mary writes in a steno notebook found at the church in her personal belongings:

"GRAND RAPIDS, MICH. JAN 1949 -Bishop Lewis called from Lansing and said he needed a worker for Pioche. He had talked with Malcolm Jones who assured him I would be able to handle this assignment. Bishop sent letter to confirm his phone call asking me to come to Christ Church.

"I was not sure I wanted to come to Nevada, but Fr. Jones assured me, 'Of course you do.' He sat down at his desk and wrote out a telegram of acceptance and said, 'Send this.'

"I left Grand Rapids in an almost new Buick – a demonstrator— with my few possessions, typewriter, sewing machine, movie projector and slide projector. I headed south thru Indiana and visited my parents in Jasper, Indiana, and arrived in Las Vegas Feb. 1, 1949, where I met Bishop Lewis at Alaska Motel."

"Feb. 1, 1949 – LAS VEGAS, NV. – THE YEAR OF THE GREAT HAY LIFT

Meet Bishop William F. Lewis at Alaska Motel – Doris Evans, proprietors. Mrs. Evans presented me with one of their beautiful 'Desert Sands' hand-made vase. Mr. Evans holds patent for method of making this pottery. The colors go completely thru the pottery.

"After dinner and visit with Bishop Lewis and discussion of my duties in Pioche and Lincoln County I spent one night in Las Vegas. The next morning I left for Pioche where I was met by Archdeacon Theodore Kerstetter. He took me to Mountain View Hotel where I spent the first three nights until church building could be heated up and made ready. For some weeks all of Miss Matz's things were placed in the bedroom, and I slept in the living room of the apartment. (Miss Matz, also a Deaconess and apparently having only one leg as reported by parishioner, Sue Lloyd Hutchings, was retiring).

"Fr. Kerstetter held the Sunday service and I met the Pioche congregation — Isabelle Godbe, Mona Scott, Bernice Roeder Cline, Agnes Cottino. These

faithful were the congregation on which I started to build a vibrant congregation."

Now, Mary does not mention anything about the town in these first few notes taken, but we must assume that she was in complete shock — Grand Rapids, Michigan, to Pioche, Nevada? The year of the great hay lift refers to a year with the highest amount of snow ever recorded in Pioche. I am amazed that she even managed to pull the grade into town with that Buick and no snow tires. My father brought his bride and me, at age two, to Pioche in late September of 1948. My mother later said that she would have left that year, but she couldn't get out of town because of the snow. In time, she began to thaw out along with the snow drifts!

Established in 1868, Pioche was named for a prominent mining financier, Francois Lewis Alfred Pioche, and was known as the wildest town in Nevada. It was said that seventy-five men died in fights over claims, money, and imagined insults before anyone died of natural causes. During the years 1871 and 1872, three out of five Nevadans who came to a violent end, did so in Pioche. Most of these unfortunates were laid to rest in Boot Hill, with tombstones sporting these epitaphs:

"Morgan Courtney, feared by some, respected by a few, detested by others."

"Shot 4 times in the Back. 1844-1873"

"Fanny Peterson, July 12, 1872. They loved til death did them part. He killed her."

James W. Hulse, in his excellent history *Lincoln County, Nevada: 1864-1909,* wrote that, *"Lincoln County deserves consideration as one of the more representative of Nevada's mining regions. Mining activity in southeastern Nevada prompted the Legislature to create the county in 1866 in order to provide it with more local government control. It was named for the recently assassinated Abraham Lincoln. From its creation until the mid-1870s, it rivaled Virginia City as the mining center of the entire western United States – particularly the very rough town of Pioche with its rich silver mines.*

"In the mid-1870s after Pioches's boom had run its course, the county declined, but mining had a revival with the Delamar strike in the early 1890s. This lasted well into the 20th century. Later, after WWII, mining revived again with the lead, zinc and tungsten mining production at Pioche and Tempiute, but was over by 1958…."

The Episcopal Church arrived in Lincoln County on September 17, 1870, on horseback when Bishop Ozi William Whitaker rode into town on his mission to bring the Episcopal Church to every mining and railroad town and Indian reservation in Nevada and Arizona. He had been ordained a priest in 1863, and was appointed Missionary Bishop in 1869, when both states were booming due to the gold and silver strikes. He later described his first service held in Pioche:

"It was in a drinking saloon, the largest room in the town. Amidst the incongruous surroundings the Services of the Church were performed in a congregation of rough miners. About one hundred and fifty persons crowded the saloon, and as many more were gathered around the door unable to gain admission." Bishop Whitaker had even covered the saloon artwork with blankets in this makeshift cathedral.

It was upon the foundation of this church planted by the missionary Bishop, that Deaconess Mary Christiana Hettler set about to serve and build a congregation, doing the rural parish ministry that she had grown to love back in the days of her Town and Country Council work. She was very prepared for her new work, as she had been seasoned by rural work in the Midwest, cathedral work in Michigan, and more than a fair amount of church politics. She had plenty of energy, which was going to be needed, because her new position required that she not only minister to the congregants living in Pioche, but also to all those living in Caliente, Tempiute, Elgin, and all potential congregants residing in the mountains, in the canyons, and on both sides of every creek in a radius of 10,637 square miles. Deaconess Mary was very accustomed to driving long distances, but mostly on flat ground in the Midwest. Driving in Lincoln County is a different matter and takes the utmost of nerve and grit, which was not lacking in our enthusiastic Deaconess.

The Pioche Record of March 17, 1949 reports:

"Deaconess Mary C. Hettler, Sunday 10:00 a.m., Sunday school, 11:00 a.m. Morning Prayer and sermon. Wednesday 7:30 p.m. mid-week Lenten service. Saturday 2:30 p.m. children's hour. Deaconess Hettler will go to Caliente on Sunday evening where she will conduct a service of evening prayer at St. Matthew's church at 8:00 p.m." One must note that Pioche and Caliente are twenty-five miles apart on Highway 93.

Mary had other handwritten notes for 1949:

(1) Vacation School at St. Bartholomew's, Ely – stayed at Hotel (John & Mary Ann Myers).

(2) Vacation school at Eureka. Stayed at Eureka Hotel. Called on parents of students one Indian family – several children – I asked for birthdays and baptism information.

(3) Vacation school Austin – Mary Ferguson and Fr. Kerstetter and I stayed with private family who had lots of cats – they also collected much old mining stuff and purple bottles.

Undated notes: *"From the time I arrived regular Sunday services were conducted in Pioche at 11 a.m and also Caliente at 9 a.m. One Sunday each month a priest came to provide Holy Communion in both places. Both congregations were very small. Neither place had a church school.*

"Each Saturday I arranged to get and show a movie for children. Everyone was invited and no charge was made. These were not religious pictures, but all were available in exchange for paying shipping costs. They were both educational and pure entertainment. This gave me an opportunity to

learn to know the children and their friends. From this activity a church school grew."

During the 1950s in Pioche, I looked forward to Vacation Bible School. Deaconess Mary, with her love and aptitude for crafts, was able to turn this week into a vibrant and fun-filled learning experience. I was especially fond of the mosaic crosses we made from small broken pieces of old plates and dishes. Mary Bradshaw Swenson remembers making pin cushions and copper rubbings, as well as the mosaics. I do remember learning how to look up the individual books inside the Bible, but this paled in comparison to the mosaic cross. Sandy Hamdorf Christensen recollects pressing leaves and flower petals between blueprint paper and glass. Our Deaconess ran a truly "blue ribbon" vacation Bible school.

The Deaconess notes further, *"Pioche had a small congregation of older women, Mona Scott, Grace Bowman, Isabel Godbe, Bernice Cleine, Leona Cheeney. Others included Bill Orr, Marion and Helen Orr, John Orr, Joan Christian and her mother Louise, Betty Heidenreich and her two daughters, Neva and Ann."*

Ann Heidenreich Henderson remembers one time when a number of the young people in Pioche were scheduled to go to a youth conference in Yerington, Nevada, which was 377 miles from Pioche, and the Deaconess was planning to drive them in her car, but she got sick and couldn't make the trip. She was so determined that these kids were going to have this experience at the youth conference that she offered her car to a bunch of teenagers and sent them off across the desert alone without an adult chaperone. Somehow they made it there and back safely. Ann is not sure if any one of them had a driver's license. We both concluded with a chuckle, "Yes, Deaconess loved young people, but she might have been a bit naïve," as were our parents. It was a special time in a small, isolated community when children were always safe to roam about.

Mary's notes continue: *"Isabel Godbe played the organ and later both Helen Orr and Joan Christian played until the good Lord took them away. Mona Scott acted as Treasurer for a number of years. Bill Orr served as warden for all the years I served. He also kept my car well-maintained. After some time a women's guild was formed who helped raise money for special projects. Bernice Cleine and Marion Orr served as Altar Guild."*

Deaconess Mary wrote in the May 1957 issue of *Cross Roads — Rural Worker's Fellowship of the Episcopal Church:* *"The County is over two hundred miles from north to south and extends from the Utah border west into the mountains as far as one can go. There is one main highway from north to south, #93, and all east and west roads are unimproved and lead only to mines or ranches. One road crossing through the county east and west will be oiled this summer and make east and west travel possible for the first time in this area of the state. The nearest railroad connection is at Caliente and a bus passes through on alternate days (except Sundays) going north one day and south the next. Hence a car is a necessity in the work and I average better than a thousand miles a month of driving.*

 "The nearest priest, Fr. Weida, is at Ely, Nevada, 109 miles to the north….Christ Church and St. Thomas Church in Las Vegas are 200 miles to the south… East and west in either direction it is now over three hundred miles to where a priest is to be found. The new road will connect us with the Church at Tonopah in the west, a distance of 205 miles across an alkali desert…..I have since learned to know many of the people who live at the end of these trails and have some twelve families to whom I send 'Home Prayer.' Some of our people serve on

the maintenance crews along the railroad, and live at those isolated sections.

"One of these families lives on the section at Elgin. The father works as a rancher during the summer and on the R.R during the winter months. The mother is a registered nurse and serves as postmistress for the section and a ranching area more than 25 miles around. They have four small children and have brought each in turn to St. Matthias to have them baptized. Elgin is some twenty miles down Rainbow Canyon and they must cross through the creek nine times to get to Caliente. When the heavy snows melt too fast or the flash floods come with the heavy rains they often have no way to get out except by flagging down a train or one of the railroad hand cars. I usually get down to visit this family two or three times a year. They usually get up about an equal number of times to make their communion at the church. The road is narrow and just clings to the canyon walls and rock slides often do great damage and block whole sections, so it takes slow and careful driving. But the welcome one receives from this isolated family makes the trip more than worthwhile, and I only regret that I can't go more often."

Mary Bradshaw Swenson was a little girl living in Rainbow Canyon near Elgin during this period of time and may have been one of the children referred to in the story just told. She remembers that since they were twenty miles of very rough terrain from a grocery store, it was vitally important to stock their refrigerator with the necessities, which meant no room for ice cream. During one summer Deaconess Mary had given her Aunt Barb all of the materials needed to conduct a summer vacation Bible school for all of the children on the nearby ranches. When graduation day came, Mary recalls, *"Here comes the Deaconess in her car crossing the creek nine times with a big gallon of hand packed ice cream for the graduation ceremonies. This meant so much to us kids to have a graduation party with ice cream; I will never forget it."* Now that's delivering God's Word at its best.

Deaconess Mary further reports in the *Crossroads Journal*, *"Sundays I leave Pioche before eight and drive to Caliente, light the fire and pick up some of the children for service. I have a service of Morning Prayer with an address suitable for the children and then drive back to Pioche for an 11:00 a.m. family service with classes for all ages following. (Cleaning the buildings, lighting fires and conducting services are all part of the regular routine of mission work. Since coming I have managed to eliminate all of the old coal wood stoves and now have oil piped in to all the stoves so the work is much simpler.) I take one day a week to visit in each of the nearby communities. Panaca and Castleton are each about twelve miles from Pioche. Castleton is our big mine and Panaca is the second Mormon settlement in the state, but we have a few families living there. The third day I go to Caliente…..The Bishop arranges for a priest to make a monthly visit to bring us our communions. Many times this means that he or the general missionary makes a trip from Reno, a round trip distance of some 900 miles, in order that we may receive the sacraments regularly."*

  It is important to note that a Deaconess could not administer Holy Communion and also could not preach. All sermons had to be read to the rural congregation from something prepared by the national church. I, for one, was bored to death with these treatises. The only one I can remember in all the years that I attended church was about Ezekiel's bones, which I found quite unusual and compelling. Deaconess Mary would not break any of these rules and never did deliver a sermon from the pulpit or administer Holy Communion to us, maintaining an emphatic loyalty to the canons of the church.

The Hamdorf family moved to Lincoln County in the late 1950s and rented a house at the Prince mine in Castleton, where Mr. Hamdorf had a contract for a construction job. Within the first month after arriving, Alice Hamdorf had a serious car accident and was in the Pioche hospital for over a month. The family was new in town with no friends and no extended family. Sandy Hamdorf Christenson, one of the three children, remembers that, *"The Deaconess visited my mother all the time in the hospital, and she and my mother became close friends, corresponding for years later after the Hamdorf family moved again. We had attended the Church of Christ in California, but after the accident, the whole family became Episcopalians and stayed in the Episcopal Church even after moving from Pioche years later."*

Deaconess Mary writes: *"Now most people take lawns and gardens for granted, but not so in Pioche. The mountain sides are rocky and bare and there is little natural vegetation except for tumble weeds, sage brush and juniper. The town is in the crotch of several mountains at an elevation of 6,500 feet. Until about four years ago, all the water came from springs, and melting snow and was collected in reservoirs and then rationed to the users in small quantities. There was only one lawn in Pioche when I arrived, and that was a very small part of the yard. There were a few small flower beds. I followed suit and planted a few spring bulbs close along the wall of the Church. Then four years ago when they piped the water from the 1200 ft. level of the big mine over the mountains I planted a lawn after raking hundreds of rocks off the mountain side. The first year the birds feasted on what seed didn't blow away, but the second year, I covered the seed with sacks, kept it well watered and got a good stand. Now more and more families are planting lawns and flowers."*

I don't know who mowed this lawn. All I know is that I and every other child and teenager who ever attended Christ Church Pioche loved to roll sideways down the steep incline of the lawn over and over again. The Deaconess had planted hollyhocks and varieties of other very hardy plants at the bottom, which provided a great stopping point when little bodies reached the end of the line.

Mary continues in her report for the *Cross Roads Journal of Rural Workers*: "But, I must tell you *about my near neighbor, a little woman over eighty who had a flower garden below me. She found it necessary to move down nearer the center of town and when she did so she hired a boy with a trailer to come and dig all the dirt from her garden and move it down to the new house. I remember thinking to myself – 'Now, I have seen everything' – but, I must admit good earth is scarce and has to be hauled in from the valley for gardens. Isolated from much of the world's busyness, television and the spots of commercial recreation and common commodities, easily available in most communities, the work of the church in a small mining camp and ranching area pays big dividends. Many persons have come to know God and for the first time learn what it really means to be one of His family in Christ. They meet a personal concern for them as persons with grateful appreciation and make vital spiritual growth. Many who had only a dim notion of the church's mission have come to a sharp and clear vision of purpose.*

"The wedding of a local nurse proved to be a real teaching instrument. Joyce was working on the staff of the local hospital and came to ask if she might be married from the Church. She was a member of the Canadian Presbyterian Church and had no family in this country, but she very much

wanted a church wedding. The nearest Presbyterian Church was in Las Vegas, two hundred miles distant. I made sure that there was nothing to prevent her having a church wedding and then arranged to have Fr. Weida of Ely give the instruction and come down for the service. Joyce chose a white satin gown with a train and had three bridesmaids and ushers. The Church was simple, but beautifully decorated. In most places this would have passed for a simple wedding, but not in Pioche. I discovered that a Church wedding was very much a novelty; the Mormon Church people have either the J.P. or one of their Bishops marry them in a home or civil ceremony. The Roman Catholics have no church building here so they must go elsewhere to have a church wedding. Most persons simply have some civil ceremony and then a reception which is the big event. Following the service there was much discussion and many questions and one churchwoman in her early thirties who has lived here all her life made the statement, 'I always thought that weddings like this only happened in the movies.' Since that time four of our Church girls have chosen to be married from the Church. Each of these services has been simpler than the first but in every case the couples have *been eager for Christian marriage and have welcomed the instruction required and given.*

"Not infrequently I am called upon to bury the dead. Sometimes a family will request the services of a priest and then I make the necessary arrangements. The Odd Fellows came to me one day and asked if I would read the burial office for Bill. He had once run the 'Beanery' where many of the miners ate but in recent years had been a ward of the county. I was also to arrange for some music and someone to sing and they in turn would dig the grave and act as the pall bearers. They were anxious that Bill have a decent burial. I secured the services of my organist and found four women who would sing a couple of the Church's hymns. We arrived at the mortuary just before the hour set for the service only to be greeted by the mortician who said, 'We have to dig a little more out of the grave. The casket won't go in.' He loaded up all the pall bearers and left for the cemetery. (I discovered later that the hole was dug 'V' shape and was big enough only at the top. We waited forty-five minutes while they blasted and dug rocks from the grave. The organist pumped away at the little reed organ. When they returned I read the service and we sang the hymns. The service completed at the mortuary, I expected that we would move on to the

cemetery, but instead the casket was thrown open and we were all invited to view the deceased. Bill had no family nor relatives and few friends so I was somewhat startled when 'Joe' began to weep copious tears. I asked if he had been a special friend and received the reply, 'No, but someone aught to cry for him.' We proceeded to the cemetery and the balance of the service went without incident.

"This doesn't begin to tell the story but I can assure you that the compensations more than outweigh the hardships of being one of God's helpers in this isolated field. Following the death of my Warden's father, his little son asked, 'Mother is Deke related to us?' 'No' replied the mother, but he still persisted 'Well, she sure acts like it.' They, too, have taken me in as a member of the family."

This reference probably refers to the Bill and Jean Orr family, who were faithful congregants for many years. Bill was the senior warden for the entire time that Deaconess Mary served, as well as the handy mechanic who kept that Buick running! Jean, who had joined the Episcopal Church as an adult while living in Pioche and had become a great friend of Mary's, later was called by the Parish and became the first woman to be ordained an Episcopal priest in the Diocese of Nevada.

Pioche was a town where many people were called by nicknames, sometimes for so many years that everyone forgot their real name. The Deaconess eventually was affectionately called "Deke" by the townsfolk, which was a compliment in Pioche, where names like "High Pockets," "White Horse," "Swede," "Abie," "Toogie," and "Shorty" were commonplace. Many miners traveled from town to town looking for the next big boom, so long term relationships weren't valued as in some other places, not to mention that many of those hard living men were leaving a past behind. Shortened names worked well for everyone. Pedigrees did not have a high priority in Pioche.

On December 20, 1951, Bishop Lewis wrote to Mary from his office in Reno, Nevada: *"First of all congratulations on your anniversary tomorrow. Your calendar of remembrance does not tell me how long you've been a Deaconess, but I know it has been a number of years of devoted faithful work. I can't tell you how much it means to me and to all of us to have you holding down that rugged southeast corner of the state and declaring the Good News by word and deed. I'm grateful to God for your coming to us and your able and faithful work. May God bless you and give you many more years of active duty. God grant that we may have the benefit of them in Nevada, too."* Mary had been a Deaconess for fourteen years and had hit her stride with confidence and strength.

In Bishop Lewis, Mary had found a true friend and a wonderful mentor. He appreciated the work she was doing and understood the value of her gifts. He knew he could leave Lincoln County in her good hands, and that with proper support from him and other clergy she could handle this mission territory. Like any good manager when you find someone with this type of competence, you provide them with support and then just step aside.

Terry Cochrane, the widow of Bishop Robert Cochrane, lived in Nevada during the 1950s while her husband served as a Curate at Trinity Episcopal in Reno and later as Vicar of St. Timothy's in Henderson. *"All of the clergy in the Diocese of Nevada during the 1950s were like one big family,"* she said. *"There weren't many of us, and we were just like a family."* In fact, Deaconess Mary was the God-mother at the baptism of the Cochrane's second son, Stephen, which was obviously an honor for Mary, as she continued to send Stephen gifts through the years even though the Cochrane family had moved away and they didn't see one another again. She had saved many pictures of Stephen, his thank you notes and Christmas cards from Terry and Robert. All of the goodwill and collegiality among the clergy and among her congregants provided Mary with a ready-made Nevada family, and it showed, as everyone remembered her during these years as being very jovial, full of laughter, and exhibiting a great sense fun.

Nov. 29, 1959 - Stephen Cochrane

The Diocese of Nevada under the leadership of Bishop Lewis was privileged and just plain lucky to have purchased eight and one-half acres of beachfront property on the east shore of Lake Tahoe. The Bishop was able to leverage the value of the former Camp Galilee situated near the bustling State Line, too close to the booming tourist and casino area, in order to purchase the new acreage near Glenbrook. He then oversaw, along with several key volunteers, the building of a small but magnificently beautiful chapel using materials from the Church in Goldfield, Nevada, which had been shuttered due to the closing of the mines in that area. Tom Magruder wrote in the February 1989 issue of the *Episcopalian*, *"While Bishop Lewis' spirit was usually in heaven, his feet were still very much on the ground. And even sometimes underground. One day an Eastern Bishop drove into the camp looking for Bishop Lewis, and he was flabbergasted to find him in a trench digging up a water line."*

With this type of a leader, of course, all of the Diocesan clergy became involved with Camp Galilee. The Bishop lived at Galilee in the summers, managing children's camps during the week and preaching on Sundays in the Chapel. Deaconess Mary was more than happy to join the group and she worked tirelessly to bring children from eastern Nevada to this special place for a great "church camp" experience.

The "groundbreaking and dedication of site" ceremony for St. John's, Glenbrook, took place in July 1947.

Mary writes: *"Summer – 1949 – First group to Galilee, Marleen Bicknell, Leo Cheeney, Diane Robinson and Pete Getker - a group of children who had never been out of Lincoln County. When we reached Lahontan Dam, they were sure we must be at Tahoe — so much water, more than they have ever seen. I acted as counselor and had one cottage plus teaching a class. 1950 – Midget camp was inaugurated. This was a great success and only a couple of homesick children, but none who had to leave camp. Classes, handwork, recreation and food kept everyone busy and happy. Every day began with Eucharist followed by breakfast. Then cabin clean up and cabin inspection. Most classes were taught by clergy or seminarians. The Bishop (Lewis) was very active in the camp programs and lived all summer in Whitaker House. I conducted classes in altar guild work. Every other week I took a group of four or five children to camp and returned a group who had already enjoyed camp."*

The trip to Camp Galilee on the eastern shore of Lake Tahoe was about 900 miles round trip each time. Bill Orr certainly had a full time job keeping that Buick running. According to the mileage records turned in for reimbursement of her automobile expense, in 1958, Deaconess Mary made five round trips to Galilee in June one in July and one in August. That's 6,300 miles traveled that summer along with eleven side trips to Carson City and two to Reno. It stands to reason that she transported at least twenty-five children from Eastern Nevada to Camp Galilee that summer alone.

Mary continues her notes about Galilee:

"Various of clergy and seminarians conducted services at Christ Church the Sundays I was in camp....While Bob (Orpew) was here we toured the countryside and found a hillside where a group of sheep had perished in 1949 – the bones were all

bleached and white. We picked up a bunch and put them in a box in trunk of my car. When we returned to camp they went too. When we arrived back at Camp we were met by Bishop Lewis, whose car would not run, so he borrowed mine just as it was, to drive into California for a late afternoon service. Since he was well known by the guard at State Line, he was waved on. When he returned we began unloading and Bob pulled out the bones. Bishop Lewis worried how he would have explained these had he have had to open the trunk for the guard. The bones later were used in a treasure hunt..."

I was lucky enough to be one of the children transported across the State in 1957 and 1958 to Camp Galilee. And, as Deaconess Mary had observed with her first group of Galilee campers, I was equally stunned by the beauty of Lake Tahoe. I can remember every part of the trip and the camp experience like it happened yesterday – worship in the Chapel, the food, singing camp songs, the cabins, swimming in the lake, talent shows, boys raiding the girls' cabins, evening prayers on the ridge overlooking the lake, commonly known as "Point Prayer," and the long ride home with no air conditioning and lots of stinky tennis shoes. Oh, I guess I don't remember the curriculum, but

Deaconess Mary was once again leading us by deeds more than with words. She took the time and the energy — and it takes a lot of energy to drive a car-load of kids from Pioche, Nevada, to Lake Tahoe to camp, and then live with them for a whole week, hoping they will have a spiritual, life-changing experience, and then drive all the way home again with the car full of over-stimulated but under-rested children.

Fortunately for me, this paradigm worked wonders. It is so difficult to express what an experience like this does for a child growing up in a rural area with very little exposure to the outside world. I remain faithful to the Galilee camping experience to this day, volunteering my time as often as possible to help others maintain this natural altar on the water facing the snow cross on the mountains afar, and to keep it available to all who wish to partake of the experience.

THE DEACONS' LAMENT

Dedicated to:

The Lord Bishop of Nevada
also known as:
Plus William Tahoe
"The Underground Bishop"

On top of Lake Tahoe,
Where bright shines the sun,
We learned our first lesson:
To be a deacon's no fun.

The Bishop drives garbage,
The Priests run the camp,
But the poor little deacons
Are worse than a tramp.

The campers go running,
While the couns'lors go free,
But the poor little deacons
Must work like a bee.

On top of Lake Tahoe,
Where winds blow all day,
The staff does their gabbing,
But the deacons must pray.

We're kidded all day long;
We're deacons, it's true.
But all Priests remember
That you're deacons too.

The Church has great wisdom.
We know that is true.
But the work that needs doing,
A deacon can't do.

The mor'l of the story
Don't try in the least
To be a poor deacon.
Make sure you're a Priest.

But if you are crazy,
You'll go on from there.
And you'll be a Bishop
And lose all your hair.

Sung to the tune of "On Top of Old Smokie".

Written at Camp Galilee for a skit - 1959

Knowing there were few clergy in the Diocese at that time, and the love that they all had for Camp Galilee, I am sure that Deaconess Mary had a great deal to do with curriculum and organization at the camp all through the 1950s. According to Mary Bradshaw Swenson, *"Deke worked year around for Camp Galilee and took many trips to Las Vegas to meet with people to plan things for the camp."*

Tempiute, in Lincoln County, is now a ghost town. It's close to Rachel, Nevada, on Route 375 and about 157 miles from Las Vegas. Silver was first discovered there in 1865, and a modest amount of silver mining went on for several years. Tungsten ore was discovered in 1916, but was not aggressively mined until 1940, when a need for it arose due to World War II. The price of tungsten rose in the early 1950s and the town grew to a population of 700, becoming one of the major tungsten producers in the nation. However, the price of the metal dropped in about 1957, and the town died, as do towns totally reliant on one employer. Episcopal services were started Nov. 29, 1953, by the Rev. Gail E. Howlett, General Missionary of Clark County, who helped to establish a thriving mission at Tempiute, where services were held two Sundays a month. However, by 1957, when the population fell in Tempiute, services were suspended there.

In the *History of the Episcopal Church in Nevada 1860-1959*, author Rolfe B. Chase writes, *"Deaconess Hettler of Pioche was probably active in this mining camp, and while the records located do not confirm it, she must have conducted some of the reported services. There were many more services reported than could be accounted for by a once or twice a month visit by Father Howlett."*

Coincidentally with the rise and fall of mining in Tempiute, Southern Nevada had just been chosen by the Federal Government as the appropriate location for above ground nuclear testing. Michon Mackedon, in her recently published book, *Bombast*, reports,

"In the wee hours of 27 January 1951, the first in a chain of events commenced, leading to Nevada's inaugural atomic weapons test, code name Able. Under the cloak of night, a nuclear capsule was transported from the Los Alamos Scientific Laboratory (now Los Alamos National Laboratory, or LANL) to a highly secure area of Kirtland Air Force Base, outside Albuquerque, New Mexico. At

Kirtland a B-50D bomber idled while the Los Alamos capsule was coupled, on board, with an assembled nuclear device; the two units, when locked together, comprised an operational atomic bomb. The B50D took off from the Kirtland airstrip, droned northwest over the Nevada border to the Las Vegas-Tonopah Gunnery Range (soon to be called the Nevada Test Site). After two practice runs over Frenchman Flat, at 5:36 a.m. the bomber released an operational weapon, which detonated in a fiery burst at 1,060 feet above ground. After a few seconds, there arose a pinkish mushroom cloud that drifted eastward. A series of echoes from the blast concussion seemed to drum the cloud out of Nevada and into Utah.

"Even as the shock waves receded and the mushroom cloud blew east, secrecy gave way under a flare of light bright enough to wake up people in Los Angeles. The public was, in an instant, sucked into a vortex of amazement, enchantment, fear, and pride – emotions that would be rekindled later that same year by the detonations of Baker, Easy, Baker-2, Fox, Sugar, and Uncle."

Deaconess Mary loved photography and even though she had few possessions, an above average camera was always one of them. When she packed up the almost new Buick and motored to Nevada with these few possessions in 1949, among them was a slide projector. Mary loved to take pictures in the desert – she had fallen in love with the desert foliage and especially desert flowers. It seems that people relocating to Nevada either fall quickly in love with the desert, or they just never quite take to it. Mary took to it in spades, and almost greater than her love for taking pictures was her love of presenting slide shows.

Now Tempiute just happens to be located next door to the east side of the Nevada Test Site – you might say an easy hike from what is commonly now known as Area 51. It is clear that Mary was ministering to the congregants in the missionary church at Tempiute, because she was also taking slides of the mushroom clouds emitted when the above ground nuclear bombs were set off. According to relatives, she also had slides of some very unusual looking aircraft. Her vantage point would have been just east of the testing area and in direct line to the movement of the mushroom clouds. She had the same feelings as all Nevadans at that time – amazed, enchanted, full of fear and at the same time full of pride at the strides our Government was taking in the nuclear arms race with the Soviet Union.

By 1959, all of Lincoln County was suffering economically. The need for its metals had declined; the mines couldn't make a profit; the County was too far off the beaten track to garner much tourism, and the population of Pioche was moving in a downward trend. The statistics of the parochial reports at St. Matthias in Caliente that year showed four communicants and a Sunday school with two teachers and nine pupils. There was no longer any need for services in Tempiute, and at Christ Church Pioche there were thirty-one communicants and no active Sunday school. Ninety services were held during the year, of which, twenty-two were Holy Communion celebrated by visiting clergy. The national Episcopal Church had still not made any changes in the requirements for Deaconesses or in the list of liturgical acts that they could and could not perform. They absolutely could not administer Holy Communion, and rural areas still needed visiting clergy to bring the sacraments to the congregants. A Deaconess could not, according to the canons of the church, take on this role.

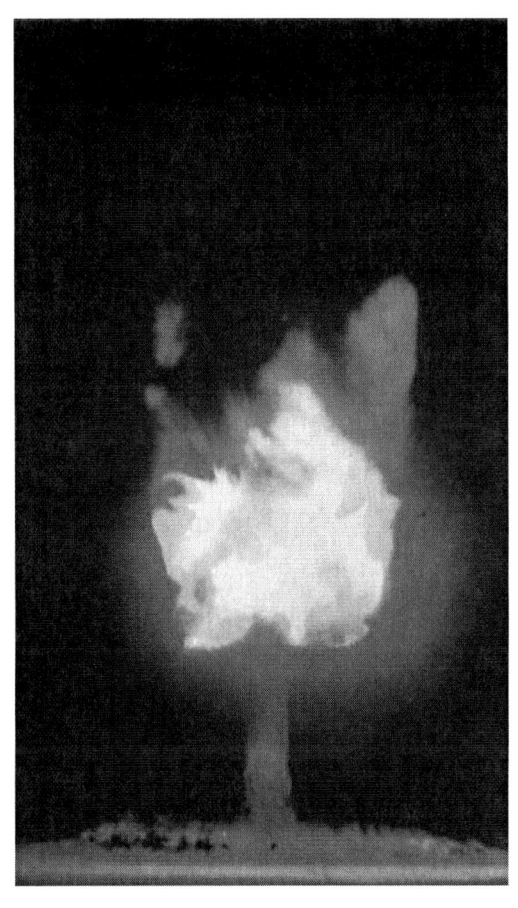

Above ground test shot

Mary's original undated slide.

Chapter 9

Love and Marriage

At some point during late 1959 or early 1960, Deaconess Mary became embroiled in some very serious issues involving a church family in the Caliente area, James (Jim) and Harriet Bradshaw. They had three children, Jane, Mary and Bill, and had been parishioners for some years. Harriet, a registered nurse, had volunteered as a camp nurse for a number of years at Camp Galilee, and she and the Deaconess had developed a close friendship.

The Bradshaw marriage was troubled and had become a vicious battleground while both partners struggled with personal demons. They eventually separated, and there were no winners, only survivors. Jim and Harriet are both deceased and have taken their individual stories to their graves. What we do know is that Jim Bradshaw at some point during the separation took the three children to his family's ranching area south of Caliente, known as Rainbow Canyon – a remote area — and that Harriet sought work in Park City, Utah.

After some months, Jim was able to get a job at the Nevada Nuclear Test Site, which required that he board on the premises during the week, putting him in need of child care. Deaconess Mary either volunteered or was asked to take the children during the week into her basement apartment in the church. Since she only had two bedrooms, she agreed to take the two girls, and Jim arranged to board his son, Bill, with a family in Pioche. Jim continued to visit the girls and Bill regularly in Pioche during the weekends.

In the latter part of her life, Deaconess Mary shared with Episcopal priest Eric Heidecker, who had become a close friend, how happy she had been during that time when she was alone with the two girls. She recounted to him where each had slept and many anecdotes about their life together. It was a very upsetting time for the children, but Mary loved being their caretaker and relished every minute she had with them.

However, in 1959, Mary's mentor and great supporter, Bishop William Fisher Lewis, left Nevada as he was elected as the Bishop Coadjutor of the Diocese of Olympia in Washington. He was consecrated there on January 6, 1960, and was replaced in Nevada by Bishop William Godsell

Wright. The new Bishop did not have the warm "hail fellow well met" type of personality that Bishop Lewis had, and according to Terry Cochrane, widow of Father Robert Cochrane, *"He just wasn't a good fit in Nevada, and I think he and my husband had words at some point."* Terry and Farther Cochrane were very close to all of the clergy, so I think her words may sum up the general consensus of the clergy at that time.

Whether it was depression over a declining ministry in Lincoln County; the loss of her mentor, Bishop Lewis, and the looming possibility that Bishop Wright might not think her ministry in rural Nevada worthy of financial support; the loneliness of listening on cold winter nights to that eastern Nevada wind howl around the sides of the basement apartment; the loss of her father November 4, 1960, and her sister, Betty, in 1958; the missed opportunity of having a husband and children (in 1960 she was 49 years old); or for all of these reasons, Deaconess Mary fell in love with James W. Bradshaw, the handsome cowboy and sometimes mining prospector, agreeing to marry him and to help raise his three children.

When Father Erick Heidecker first met Mary Hettler Bradshaw, he was a new young priest in the

Diocese of Nevada, and Mary was aging. He inquired of her, *"And, what does your husband do?"* Mary replied, *"He is a prospector."* Erick naively responded, *"Oh, I understand that some of the mines are opening up again."* Mary looked straight at him and said, *"In Nevada, prospector means you're out of work."* From such a dubious starting point, Father Erick and Mary continued a dialog and eventually became fast friends. In time, Mary opened up completely to him and used him as a sounding board for her end–of-life reflections. She explained to him, *"I always needed to be needed."* Erick recalled, *"She said she realized she never married Jim. She married an image of him that was in her head. And then later, when he proved not to be the saintly and innocently wronged father, sacrificing all for his children, she became angry and resentful with him for that. In the year the two girls were living in the church with her, a real high point in her life by the way, Jim did sort of present himself as that image, but looking back she would laugh and say he never really was that good of an actor and she bought into it so completely only because she so desperately wanted to. She saw only what she wanted to see. And, in the long run, none of it worked out like her fantasy."*

Perhaps, Jim only saw what he wanted to see, as well. Affairs of the heart have a very circuitous path at times, and even Deaconesses are not immune to being tossed and turned by those turbulent waters.

In May 1961, Deaconess Mary told Bishop Wright of her plans to marry Jim Bradshaw, at which time he told her that her services would no longer be needed and to turn in her starched wimple, collar and cuffs. According to Mary's records, the exact date was May 15, 1961. Jane Bradshaw Smart, the eldest of the three Bradshaw children, recalls that Mary had a week to move out of the church, and she went to stay with Rev. Malcolm Jones (the rector at Christ Church Las Vegas) and his wife, Betty, until there could be a wedding – Jim and Harriet were still married, but in the process of divorce. Rev. Malcolm Jones was later shot and killed in Las Vegas by a deranged parishioner.

On Oct. 14, 1961, the day after the divorce, James W. Bradshaw and Mary Christiana Hettler were married in Las Vegas, Nevada. The two daughters were with their mother that day and did not attend, so they have no knowledge as to details of the wedding. Son Bill, age 8, did attend, but cannot remember the service. He does remember the dinner afterwards at the famous Showboat Hotel in Las Vegas. He thinks that Betty Jones was there and was probably a witness. Since Jim was a divorced man, I doubt that an Episcopal Church wedding could have been performed, especially under the reign of the "oh, so angry" Bishop William Godsell Wright, so it was undoubtedly a civil ceremony.

Always using her abilities to stretch resources, Mary had saved some money during her years in Pioche, and she had received some inheritance money, enough to build a new house on the Bradshaw ranch, a house that a family could be proud of. In 1960, according to the parochial reports, Mary was paid $3,300 per year, with the parish actually paying only $35 of that total, and the rest coming from the national church's missionary fund.

She wrote to all of her friends and her family on October 25, 1961:

Dear friends,

Many of you have known for some time that Jim and I planned to be married, to others this news will come as a complete surprise. This has been a busy summer for all of us while we made preparations and plans.

We are living on a ranch, part of a larger ranching operation owned by Jim's father. Here we have built a new four bedroom home of cinderblock. It is 30' by 40' and has a large porch and fireplace in addition.

We have three lovely children. Jane the eldest is thirteen and in the eighth grade. She is an ardent reader and loves horses and is saving any pennies to own one of her own. Mary Lou is an eleven year old sixth grader. She excels in Math, clowning and climbing. She reached the top-most fruit during the canning season. She has four cats and would like a dozen or so more. Billy is eight and all boy. He is constantly with his father and a good worker and learning all that there is to know about the ranch. He has two dogs, a Collie and an Australian shepherd. The children also have six rabbits and six ducks.

In addition to the house we have also built a large reservoir which is 100 feet square. This will irrigate our alfalfa field and provide a swimming pool in the summer months. It is five feet deep. We hope to stock it with bass and catfish.

Another week should see a lawn in around the house and later this fall we plan to put a good sized orchard in below and to the north of the house. There will be a garden next year and chickens and a milk cow in due time. Fences and additional buildings all to be built in due time.

At present Jim is working in Caliente on the State School for Girls which is under construction there. This doesn't give him much time for work on the ranch. By summer we hope to have a hundred head of cattle which we will run under our own brand. It is all very thrilling and exciting for each and all of us. Hunting Season is in full swing and here in the mountains there is lots of game – deer, quail, dove.

Our love to you and yours,

Mary and Jim

James W. Bradshaw was from an old Nevada ranching family. His grandfather, James Webster Bradshaw, rode horseback from Missouri to southeastern Nevada and settled there in 1873, purchasing land from Ben Padgett in Rainbow Canyon at Elgin with his share of the $10,000 he and Joseph Conaway realized from the sale of their mine known as *Atlantis*. Jim's father, Reuben

Bradshaw, used squatters' rights to purchase a ranch in the canyon for $70, which included a house; he married Helen Leavitt, and had seven children, with James being the oldest. According to Don Bradshaw, Jim's brother, their father, Reuben, *"always ranched, running about a 100 head of cows, was the proprietor of a small store in Rainbow Canyon, and was always prospecting for ore around the ghost town of Delamar and around the Pennsylvania District. He was able to make a living for his wife and seven children only by keeping all of these activities going at the same time."*

Jim received a high school diploma as did his other siblings by boarding with families in the nearby towns during the school year. He joined the Army after high school and fought in the Battle of the Bulge during World War II.

"Reuben, our father, had purchased the old Barnett place for back taxes for $400 – it was 160 acres – and later he deeded that parcel over to Jim," said Don Bradshaw. This was the ranch where Jim Bradshaw and Deaconess Mary settled, built a house, and started to make their life together.

Rainbow Canyon is stunningly beautiful throughout the year. Light bounces off of the high red cliffs creating prisms of every color of the rainbow; and as the sun passes across the horizon, the colors change continually and are different again according to the season. Unlike the rocky soil of Pioche, thirty miles to the north in the mountains, Rainbow Canyon is located at a much lower elevation, with a great creek running through it, leaving sediment that is constantly feeding the soil, making it rich enough to grow alfalfa for grazing cattle. This canyon also provided the best route for the Union Pacific Railroad to wind its way from Los Angeles through Las Vegas to Salt Lake City.

There were several men who first arrived in the Canyon in the 1870s along with James Webster Bradshaw. Charles Cuverwell and James A. Ryan arrived about the same time and purchased neighboring ranches. According to Kathryn Wilkes Duffin in her book, *Caliente Settlers*, "*During the 1894 to 1909 boom in Delamar, Mr. Ryan had a contract to furnish beef to the camp. Two beeves were slaughtered daily, quartered, wrapped and hauled by wagon to Delamar. Mr. Ryan dried the hides and shipped them in bundles on the train to a tannery in Los Angeles, California.*" He later deeded a part of his ranch to the Nevada State

Parks to be utilized as a state park, which is now Kershaw Ryan State Park.

Many of the ranches in Rainbow Canyon are still run by descendants of these early settlers. "The Canyon," as it is referred to by natives of Lincoln County, is and has been for almost one hundred and fifty years populated by ranchers, cowhands, mining prospectors, and railroad workers, and a few outlaws. Most of the population was Caucasian, but some were Native Americans of several different tribes. This mix resulted in a very interesting confluence of traditions. The canyon is only about thirty miles long before the land flattens out into a desert playa. It is rich in beauty, wildlife, like deer and wild horses, and culture. It is an interesting subset of a very sparsely populated larger area, and its inhabitants need each other for survival, as the creek can rise to a dangerous level at a moment's notice when the sky opens up unexpectedly. So, these different traditions have learned how to live together in harmony through the changing seasons.

The ranchers sometimes work on the railroad when ranch work is slow. The Native Americans also ranch or work as hands on the other ranches, or sometimes work for the railroad; and the railroaders enjoy the sight of the ranchers and prospectors along their route and know most of them by name. The outlaws were able to stay very well hidden in the small caverns high up on the canyon walls, gaining an unobstructed view of anyone who might approach.

It is in this setting that Deaconess Mary packed away her starched wimple and cuffs and became Mrs. James W. Bradshaw. Having spent her early childhood on a ranch near Lubbock, Texas, and having visited the ranches in the canyon many times, she understood what she was getting into with ranch life and she took to it with vigor. Never afraid of hard work, Mary rolled up her sleeves and worked tirelessly cooking, cleaning, helping with the animals and with any other work that was required.

In fact she relished her new role as ranch wife even if she was a *"full twenty miles from the nearest light bulb,"* said Mary Bradshaw Swenson. Deaconess Mary remembered that the ranches she had grown up on in Texas often had a dinner bell that the cook would ring to call in the ranch hands for meals. She contacted her sister Helen and asked her to look for one of those bells. According to Helen's niece, Anita, Helen dutifully went on a mission to find a proper Texas dinner bell, which she did find on their Uncle Cash's ranch and had the bell sent to Elgin, the post office which served the neighboring ranches. Bill Bradshaw, Mary's step son is now the proud keeper of the Texas dinner bell.

During this period the railroad had hired a number of Navajo men to work maintaining the railroad tracks up and down the canyon. The living conditions provided for these Native Americans were basically lean-to types of structures next to the tracks. Navajo men had come up from the reservations in Arizona and or New Mexico to take these jobs and generally there were not too many women with them, but occasionally there were a few. Mary, of course, with her sense of ministry and always on the look-out for the disadvantaged, befriended the Navajos in the canyon. On one particular day she was visiting a Navajo family when a very pregnant Navajo woman started into labor. All of the Navajo men looked at Mary like "*do something*," so Mary delivered the baby. Later Mary gave a Navajo rug to her Senior Warden, Bill Orr, who is since deceased. His daughter, Barbara, now has the rug. We can only surmise that the rug may have been given to Mary as a gift for delivering the baby or for some other good deed bestowed upon the Indians.

These Navajos added rich color to the already beautiful landscape in Rainbow Canyon. One of the ranchers told my father about a time when several of the ranchers had been chasing wild Mustangs with the objective of catching a few to tame and use on the ranches. They had been successful in their hunt and captured a number of horses. One old gray Mustang stallion in particular appeared to be more wild-eyed and battle scarred than the others, and the ranchers had decided that he was just not a good prospect for breaking and probably would not make a very good work horse regardless of how much time they put into him. So they offered the horse and corral space to the Navajos, who graciously accepted. Then the rodeo began, which was always enjoyed by everyone in the canyon regardless of race, sex or color. One Navajo lassoed the horse and started to walk the horse around the corral holding the rope very tight about the horse's neck. This went on for some time with the horse rearing, snorting, and bucking toward all four corners of the corral, but the Navajo kept the rope tight, and in fact, would give it an extra twist cutting off the horse's air when needed to gain the necessary respect from the stallion. Eventually, the second Navajo was able to get on the horse's back, and the walk continued with more rearing, snorting, and bucking by the Mustang and more neck tightening by the Navajo. Then after considerable more time, the third Navajo entered the corral with a broom and followed behind the parade, striking the horse on his back legs every so often when he tried to kick or cease walking. It was a great day in the canyon with lots of hoots, hollering, and leg slapping by all of the ranchers.

A week or so later the Navajos were observed with that old gray Mustang in the back of a pickup truck with no side boards, and they were on their way back to Ship Rock, New Mexico. Mission accomplished with all parties satisfied. The Navajos had a new horse, and the ranchers had had one heck of a rodeo!

Horses were a part of the fabric of rural Nevada then, and still now to a certain extent. During the 1950s and 60s, I recall that most people owned a Mustang if they had any desire or need for a horse. My dad had no need for a horse, but he sure did have a desire. I was lucky to have been old enough to remember one excursion taken with several families to chase some Mustangs in the flats somewhere between Pioche and Ely. A small Cesna airplane was used to strafe a wild band of horses, running them into a box canyon, where a camouflaged fence with an open gate awaited. As soon as the horses were safely inside the canyon, one or two men would close the gate and the horses were captured. Each family participating was entitled to one horse on that day. Our family chose a bay horse, which I promptly named "*Shorty*" – I can only guess he was slightly shorter than the other horses. My dad kept asking me if I wanted to pick a more glamorous name, but I was certain that Shorty was the best name, and Shorty it was. I like the smell of horses, and I absolutely think they are one of God's most exquisite works of art. I'm not opposed to feeding or grooming them, but riding them is a different matter for me. Therefore, with the exception of deer season, it seemed like my dad and I spent much more time trailering Shorty to different pastures and corrals for grazing during the changing seasons than we did riding him. But, he was our Mustang and we both loved him. Shorty spent the winters in Rainbow Canyon on the Ballow Ranch, so once a year we hauled him from Pioche down to the canyon and back again in the spring. On one of these trips, my dad was using a good horse trailer, but a not-so-good hitch. He kept asking me to turn around every so often and check on how the trailer was riding. I checked several times and all was OK. On the third check, I said, *"Daddy, the trailer is gone!"* Of course, Dad was horrified, as the trailer had come unhitched and rolled off the side of the road. We thought surely that Shorty was injured or killed, but he was not with the trailer. In fact, he was nowhere to be seen. A week later, however, Shorty was spotted running with his Mustang buddies across the flat below Pioche. He was captured a second time by my dad and a few friends, and back into our custody came Shorty. He was one tough Mustang!

Chasing Mustangs was also a sport of the ranchers in Rainbow Canyon, but with the high canyon walls, could be a much more dangerous sport. They used the same principle of running the wild horses into a box canyon, only they had to do this on horseback up and down the canyon walls. My dad tells in his book, *High Desert Tales*, of chasing Mustangs with the Henrie boys who owned a neighboring ranch south of the Bradshaws' ranch. Roscoe Wilkes writes, *"I had earlier observed the terrain where the chase would begin. It was sagebrush, dry ditches (gullies included), a dry creek bed and rocks. Yes, there were rocks, some as large as a wheelbarrow, some the size of a basketball, others the size of a cantaloupe and many smaller...This chase had an all consuming mission to capture Gray Ghost. It must have been near midnight when Paul whispered, 'They're coming in--They're coming in and Gray Ghost is with them.' We quietly saddled our horses and carefully approached the crucial area. As the horses emerged from the water, saw us and started to run, someone yelled, 'build to 'em.' The chase was on."*

This was an area filled with the spirit of the Wild West and it was beautiful, but the realities of trying to make a living there were pressing in on Jim and Mary Bradshaw. According to Don Bradshaw, Jim's brother, *"Jim and Mary were running about seventy five head of cows, and there was no way that anyone could make a ranch pay on seventy five head."* The ranch just was not big enough, and their plans started to unravel. The two older girls, Jane and Mary, who had loved the Deaconess growing up, were now very hurt by their parents' divorce, and just did not want anything to do with this new marriage. After a year, the two girls moved to be with their grandmother, who was living in Park City, Utah. Billy wanted to stay with his father, made his peace with the situation, and lived with his dad and Deke, as the kids called her, until he graduated from high school.

Mary Bradshaw Swenson remembers Deke as being, *"very humble and forgiving; a woman who never gave up hope. She never held a grudge against me even though we had some bad times between us. She had the fortitude and the work ethic of a pioneer. She would take whatever little she had and make it into something better. She saved everything and turned it into something else. Deke wasn't a really warm woman, but she really tried her hardest with us kids."*

After about 10 years, Jim and Mary realized there was no way to make this ranch profitable no matter how hard they worked; they were clearly going broke. So they put the place up for sale and eventually sold it in 1971 to a retired FBI agent, who would use it more as a gentleman's ranch, rather than a working ranch. They rented the old "Elgin schoolhouse," from the School District. It was a three-room structure originally built by Reuben Bradshaw for the education of his large family, and they lived there for several years while they both looked for other work.

All during these years, Jim continued to struggle with alcohol addiction – drying out several times, but always relapsing. This, of course, had ramifications for their marriage. Mary was ten years older than Jim when they married, and the marriage occurred directly on the tail of a tumultuous divorce. That, coupled with the stress of trying to make a success of a ranch that was doomed from the start meant the marriage would not go well. Due to these many frustrations, and his own inner turmoil, Jim treated Mary quite badly, attested to by his own brother and sister. Betty Bradshaw Foley said, *"He was my own brother, and I loved him very much, but you couldn't live with the guy."*

Unfortunately, another tragedy struck the family in 1964, when Mary was stricken with breast cancer. She had to undergo a double radical mastectomy. Mary would have been fifty-three, a time when statistically breast cancer is more likely to strike, but we must also remember that she had most certainly been exposed to radiation from the above-ground testing at the Nevada Test Site all through the 1950s. We don't know how many different shots she photographed, standing outside as the mushroom clouds moved east over the Tempiute area and the Bradshaw ranch, but we do have proof positive of her presence at one above ground shot as evidenced by the photograph that she took from what appears to be about ten miles away.

Jim and Mary eventually moved to Caliente to be closer to jobs. Mary realized that St. Matthias, the Episcopal Church in Caliente, was vacant and probably would not be used again. She negotiated with the Diocese of Nevada to purchase the building using funds that her sister, Helen, had been managing. She and Jim then remodeled the building, turning it into a cozy home. The house, however, remained in the name of Helen Dodson. Mary found work at the new Nevada State Girls Training Center, which had been built outside of Caliente in the early 60s. Getting back into the work force and being able to do something she considered worth-while was very good for Mary. However, she was attacked by one of the girls who was in residence, and so this job did not end well. Mary was having trouble finding her way back into the service of others, which always dictated her direction. But, the Holy Spirit was not yet through with Deaconess Mary, and she was not through with it.

At some point during these years, Mary tried to collect from the church pension fund. This was always a very cloudy area in the Deaconess program. A resolution had passed at the Chicago Diocesan convention of February 1931, petitioning the national church to inaugurate a pension system for Deaconesses. The Deaconesses were in an awkward position, as they were ineligible to benefit from the Church Pension Fund designed for priests, and unwilling to be included in a pension system for lay church workers. The Deaconess Retiring Fund had never grown to any great size. It was not supported well by the church as a whole, and depended largely on contributions of the Deaconesses themselves, who had very little income to contribute. The Deaconesses were a rapidly aging group, and concern for the many impoverished retired Deaconesses was often expressed among those who were still working. At first Mary was told that the Deaconesses could only apply for this pension based on need, which Mary was trying to substantiate. However, her sister, Helen, the accountant, had read about recent changes in the pension laws, and she went to work on challenging the system. According to Mary's niece, Anita El-Jamal, Helen prevailed, and Mary was able to access one of the established pension plans of the Church.

Also, in the late 1970s, Mary and several other Lincoln County concerned citizens, including Yuri Setzer of Panaca, were successful in establishing a new transportation system for Lincoln County, which was badly needed in this remote area, especially by senior citizens no longer able to drive the long distances to Las Vegas or to Cedar City, Utah, for medical services.

In the April 1990 issue of *Nevada Rural Connection,* we read: *"Lincoln County Transportation, which had its beginnings in 1978, is the oldest UMTA Section 18 system in the state. It is also the only bus system in Lincoln County.* (In 1978, when the transportation system was instituted, Mary would have been sixty-seven years old, and by 1990 when this article was written, she was seventy-nine and still working.)

"Under the guidance of project director, Mary Bradshaw, this very rural transit system is preparing to take on a new challenge — providing transportation to both visitors and employees of the new women's prison scheduled to be built in Pioche, 175 miles north of Las Vegas. Prior to the

final vote being taken, Mary Bradshaw was invited to speak before the Interim Finance Committee in Carson City regarding available transportation options. She is quoted as saying, 'One of the reasons the services provided by Lincoln County Transportation are so important, both to county residents and to the prison, is that the Caliente based system and the neighboring communities of Alamo, Panaca and Pioche are so isolated it's just plain difficult to get anywhere from there without your own transportation. Many residents are without that luxury. We have no shopping per se,' explains Mary. 'We have only one drug store in the entire county, one paved airport, one Amtrak station and no taxi service. As far as medical care, we do have two general practitioners – but one of them only works three days a week.'"

Our Mary had a new ministry in the field of transportation. She had written most of the grants to get this system going, and she loved every minute of it. She was once again helping the disadvantaged, and she was "on the road again," at least in spirit. Deaconess Mary loved her wheels, and the Holy Spirit had given her a new set of tires. She did not drive this bus, but she was in charge of the bus, where it went and on what day, and that was good enough for Mary. There were also necessary business trips to Carson City and to Las Vegas to administer this state-funded program. She loved this job, and it was tailor–made for her.

Navajo rug

Given by Mary to Bill Orr, Sr. Warden Christ Church

Mary and Jim Bradshaw

Chapter 10

The Church Was Blind But Now It Sees

In 1970, at the General Convention of the Episcopal Church, the following action was taken: *"Acting on the recommendation of the Lambeth Conference of 1968, the General Convention formally declared that women who have been admitted to the Order of Deaconesses in the past with the laying-on-of hands and prayer are within the Diaconate. The Convention then proceeded to repeal Canon 50, 'On the Deaconesses,' and to enact a new Canon (III.26), 'Of Women in the Diaconate.' The new Canon describes a Diaconate which is the same for women as for men."*

As regards to Deaconess Mary, this meant that women and men were both now to be called "Deacons" and would operate under the same rules – both could be married. Father Erick Heidecker says Mary was already regarding herself this way. *"She had started in recent years to think that she was ordained as a deaconess, not just 'set apart,' and that renouncing orders was a much bigger deal than just leaving a job, which is originally what she thought she was doing when she resigned in 1961. She also saw being a deacon as something important, more important than being an old-style deaconess."*

At some point after the 1970 action by General Convention, Bishop Frensdorf, who replaced Bishop Wright, approached Mary about considering a reinstatement to the Diaconate. Initially, Mary was still hurt and bruised from the actions of Bishop Wright when he deposed her. She didn't want any part of it, and she turned him down several times. However, as more women moved into the Diaconate, and with more introspection, she began to realize that perhaps there was some theological merit to Bishop Wright's actions, even though his methods were appalling.

In 1986, after the untimely plane accident in which Bishop Frensdorf was killed, Bishop Zabriskie was consecrated, and he contacted Mary regarding a reinstatement. By that time, she was starting to view the meaning of that title in a different way. This time she accepted his invitation and on March 31, 1987, Bishop Stewart Zabriskie officially restored Mary Christiana Hettler Bradshaw to the *"Ministry of the Diaconate." "This was one of the happiest days of her life,"* said her stepdaughter, Mary Bradshaw Smart. According to Father

Heidecker, "*She didn't make a big deal out of it, but she was very insistent that she was to be called deacon, not deaconess, after her reinstatement. There never was a Deaconess Bradshaw after that time. She was definitely Deacon Bradshaw.*" The name Deke was reserved only for longtime friends and relatives).

Restoration to ministry of the Diaconate

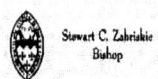

Stewart C. Zabriskie
Bishop

NOTICE OF RESTORATION
to the
MINISTRY OF THE DIACONATE

This is to certify that, acting under Title IV, Canon 13, of the Canons of the Episcopal Church, all of the conditions having been duly and satisfactorily complied with, I have this day restored to the Order of Deacons

MARY HETTLER BRADSHAW

thereby terminating the sentence of removal placed upon her, then as Deaconness, by the Rt. Rev. William G. Wright in May 1961, and to be effective 30 March 1987.

Stewart C. Zabriskie
Bishop of Nevada

31 March 1987

Post Office Box 6357 • 2390 West Seventh Street • Reno, Nevada 89513 • Telephone (702) 747-4949

On December 15, 1987, Mary writes to Bishop Zabriskie:

Dear Bishop,

I am still trying to grasp the idea of "total ministry."

Since my ordination and/or Setting Apart as a Deaconess, I never remember a time when I was able to divorce service, worship, and availability in the work of evangelism.

To put ministry into a time frame is very difficult. I have assisted at the Eucharist five times in Pioche and read lessons or the Gospel at other times.

In a practical way I have altered altar linen to fit new standing altar. Made several small linens and secured two flannel covers to go under fair linen.

Being a Deacon means continuity of service with deep devotion to our Lord. I cannot begin to tell you how much it means to me to be reinstated. Thank you.

Faithfully yours,

Mary C. Bradshaw

p.s. The enclosed clipping sounds to me like an ideal place to check out for a mission.

We don't know what kind of mission she was referring to, but we certainly know Mary well enough by now to know that she certainly had spotted some ill in the world or group of people in need of social services and God's word – and a good bishop would do well to take note!

In spite of the incredible injustices which had befallen her personally and professionally, it is clear from this letter that Mary could once again see nothing but blue sky ahead of her and all she needed was a good Buick to carry her forth on the next mission. It's quite obvious that retirement was not an option for our newly reinstated Deacon.

And, as for me, I have arrived at a place of deep spiritual contentment, often seeing differing theological viewpoints as more of a hindrance to salvation than as a help. But, attending church regularly does help to keep me centered, and my love for the Episcopal manner of religious expression continues. With Mary as my spiritual guide (yes, she is still with me), I see blue sky every day, and I just keep my hands firmly on the wheel as I trust the Holy Spirit knows the road.

On April 26, (probably 1987), Mary received a letter with the signature "Madeline," – which most certainly was written by Madeline Dunlap, who is listed as a Chase House alumnae in a 1937 brochure.

"It just can't be us who were graduated fifty years ago! Must be someone else. Frankly, my time is busier than before I was 62, and went off to do – street work – with the Quakers. Frances Z. took the wonderful news of your restoration to the diaconate to the RFD meeting this past week. Was just going through my card file of – pre -79 – and find there are so many in 80s, plus a sturdy crew of 90ers. Well, I'm just 6 months behind you.

"Nuf for this time, lots of love and joy over your being accepted in the minds of the – whatever we call them, who fail to understand that once the Episcopal hands rested on our heads, there is no erasure by humans."

Madeline Dunlap and Mary Hettler

On their way to Chase House benefit at

Edgewater Beach Hotel – November 6, 1935

Cancer returned to Mary in about 1991 – this time lung cancer. She was tended to at her home during her final illness by her husband, Jim, and her stepson, Bill, who left his job in Las Vegas to come home to Caliente to nurse her, sleeping many nights on the floor of her bedroom to be close at hand. Upon her passing on March 18, 1992, she was laid to rest at the Caliente Veterans Cemetery. Jim died in 1997 and is buried next to Mary. For better and for worse, the Deaconess and the cowboy stayed married until Mary's death.

The spirit and the ways of handling life's mysteries, joys and misfortunes by Mary Christiana Hettler live on in the hearts of the many folks who were privileged to have walked a few steps by her side.

Acknowledgments

It has taken a multitude of persons clearing brush to blaze the trail for me, so that I could write this book. First and foremost was our heroine, Deaconess Mary Hettler, who was so filled with the love of God, such an optimistic belief in her fellowman, and the courage to live her life in accordance with her principles, that it made my work easy and joyful.

I must thank my dad for sharing his great love for Nevada and the Wild West with me, and my mother for encouraging me to take a look at what else might be out there beyond our borders.

My aunt Kathryn introduced me to great literature and then, as any good English teacher would, made prodigious use of her red pen on my papers, as she held all of her students to a high standard.

I thank all members of the Bradshaw and the Hettler/ Dodson families for putting their trust in me to write this personal story about their family member. That took a blind leap of faith, as none of them knew me. And, this story would have been a ten page research paper had it not been for my friend and fellow parishioner, Jean Norman, who graciously agreed over a cup of coffee to read my first draft and then emphatically told me that this story needed to be a book. Jean has guided me through multiple revisions, monitoring the progress in a way that definitely pulled the best from me.

Lastly, if it were not for my husband, Darryl Martin, the book would have no cover, no title, and would be single-spaced type on 8 ½ X 11 paper with one staple on the top left corner. His patience with my technological neediness is beyond human, and his encouragement and advice on all matters of what must have been a million details has been invaluable. This project has taken one year to bring to fruition, and Darryl was there with words of encouragement from the first interview until the final sentence was written, absolutely refusing to allow me to get discouraged, confused, or lazy, as we both share a firm belief that Mary Hettler's story needed to be told, and that somehow I was chosen to be her vehicle.

Persons Interviewed

Jane Bradshaw Smart – Boise, Idaho – Stepdaughter of Mary

Mary Bradshaw Swenson – Salt Lake City, Utah – Stepdaughter of Mary

Bill Bradshaw - Caliente, Nevada – Stepson of Mary

Betty Bradshaw Foley – Las Vegas, Nevada – Sister to James Bradshaw

Don Bradshaw – Las Vegas, Nevada – Brother to James Bradshaw

Terry Cochrane – Seattle, Washington – Friend to Deaconess , widow of Father Robert Cochrane , And mother to Stephen Cochrane who was Mary's Godson

Sandy Hamdorf Christiansen – Boulder City, Nevada – former parishioner of Christ Church Pioche

Carl Frederick Dodson – Jasper, Indiana – Nephew of Mary

Anita Dodson El-Jamal - Houston, Texas – Niece of Mary

Rusty Fortier – Las Vegas, Nevada – former parishioner of Christ Church Pioche

Father Erick Heidecker – Episcopal priest in Nevada and friend of Mary's in her later years

Ann Heidenreich Henderson – Las Vegas, Nevada – former parishioner of Christ Church Pioche

Kathy Hiatt – Pioche, Nevada – current Deacon serving at Christ Church Pioche

Sue Lloyd Hutchings – Pioche, Nevada – long time parishioner of Christ Church Pioche

Barbara Orr – Escondido, California – former parishioner of Christ Church Pioche and daughter of Jean and Bill Orr

Jean Orr – former Priest serving at Christ Church Pioche and widow of Bill Orr, Senior Warden for all the years Mary served at Christ Church

Yuri Setzer – Panaca, Nevada – former co-worker of Mary at the Lincoln County Transportation System

Sources

Averett, Walter R*.," Through the Rainbow Canyon," Grand Junction, Colorado* 1995

Chase, Rolfe B.," *History of the Episcopal Church in Nevada* – 1860-1959," Tucson, Arizona 2000

Donovan, Mary Sudman, "*A Different Call – Women's Ministries in the Episcopal Church 1850-1920,*"Morehouse-Barlow, Wilton, Ct. 1986

Duffin, Kathryn, *"Caliente Settle*rs," Caliente, Nevada, 2002

Mackedon, Michon, "*Bombast , Spinning Atoms in the Desert*", Black Rock Institute Press, Reno, Nv.2010

Menaul, Marjorie, "*Deaconess Training in Chicago 1917-1970,*" Dec. 5, 1988

Wilkes, Roscoe, "*High Desert Tales – From the Not So Wild West*," Boulder City, Nevada 2010

✠ In the Name of the Father, and of the Son, and of the Holy Ghost. Amen.

We do Certify:

That, after the example of the Holy Apostles, and in accordance with the universal practice of the Holy Catholic Church, by the laying on of our hands, we did administer to

Karen Even Wilkes

THE SACRAMENTAL RITE OF

Confirmation

wherein were conveyed the Sevenfold Gifts of the Holy Spirit; which administration was on October 19, 19 57

in Christ Church,

Pioche, Nevada , in the

MISSIONARY DISTRICT OF NEVADA

(Signed) +Wm Fisher Lewis

The Bishop of Nevada

Presented by the Rev. Deaconess Mary C. Fettler